Clinging to the Rails

A whirlwind train trip across Europe

Hi! Thanks for opening
this book! Please take it
on your travels and pass it on!

Maybe let me know where
it has been?

Thanks!

Chris

@cpambrose

Clinging to the Rails

A whirlwind train trip across Europe

Chris Ambrose

ISBN 978-0-9564473-2-6

Published by Chris Ambrose

Cover design by Sophie Adams-Foster

Trains are great. They are a fast, comfortable and scenically engaging way of delivering you to some of the most exciting places in the world.

...if they show up. *Reggio Calabria, Italy, October 2013.*

...and if they haven't knocked down the station. *Tirana, Albania, November 2013.*

...and if the person you're travelling with hasn't just gotten on the wrong train and left you with their luggage. *Nagoya, Japan, December 2013.*

About the author

This is where authors like to tell you how great they are and how much they've achieved, whilst referring to themselves in the third person. So here goes...

Chris was born in London. He is left handed, although he does most things with his right hand, such as operating scissors and waving (although he is wise enough never to do these two things simultaneously). He has his 10 metre swimming badge, as well as his 25 metre swimming badge, which he inadvertently earned after getting into the wrong end of the swimming pool on the way to start the 10 metre swim. Chris also gained his Cub Scout *Collectors* badge for stamp collecting. He has never collected stamps, but he once owned a folder that had some stamps in it. Chris currently lives above a Polish-run hairdressers in North London. Right now he thinks he can hear a mouse in the kitchen. He'll keep you posted.

@cpambrose

Clinging to the Rails

A whirlwind train trip across Europe

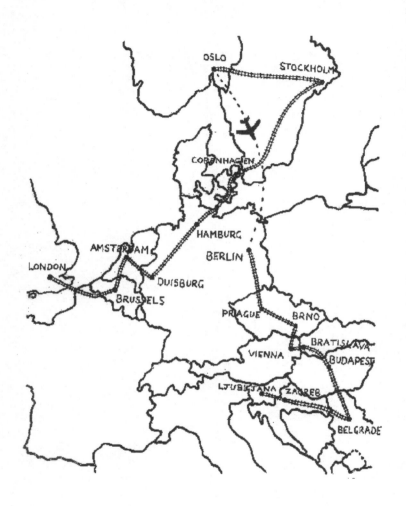

My head jerked against the back of the seat. The coarse grain of the harsh commercial fabric rubbed painfully against my nose and cheek. The cold, bitter air sent shivers through my extremities as I slowly tried to adjust to the dark surroundings. I had no idea what time it was, but the juddering had stopped. The reverberations through my torso and the low grumbling of the engine had stopped. Everything had stopped. Everything, except a sharp, slapping sensation against my right leg. As I gradually regained consciousness I started to turn. Well, as much as I could. Pain surged through my left hand side. I was sprawled out across the seats, my hands trapped somewhere behind me, my legs semi-coiled to retain any warmth my weary body could muster. Through the darkness the anguished Hungarian wailing grew in volume until it dominated my thoughts with ear-piercing clarity. That was until the heavy footsteps cut them short. There was a flicker of movement in my peripheral vision. My neck was bent awkwardly as I strained to come to terms with what was happening. Suddenly there was silence. The wailing had stopped abruptly. The door was then forcefully thrust aside to reveal a silhouette, faintly outlined by a dim, tungsten glow. The looming shape of a heavily built figure filled the doorway. The only sound now was heavy breathing: *my* heavy breathing. The figure turned slowly towards me, the faint light source from behind briefly catching on something metallic to its lower right side. The barrel of a gun.

Chapter 1

London, England

'Please be aware that due to signal problems on the line there will be delays to this service' came the voice, spluttering out of the train's tinny pa speakers above.

I pulled out an earphone to catch the tail end of the announcement. A few heavy sighs echoed around the carriage, accompanied by the thud of heads bumping despondently against adjacent windows. A young professional in a slightly dishevelled suit on the other side of the aisle muttered an expletive into his newspaper, while a middle-aged woman tutted.

It's not really what you want after a long, tiring day at work, but I don't suppose it was intentional. It did seem a shame that they had waited until we were all tightly packed onto the train before revealing this information to us, though, so we were now trapped, bumbling awkwardly along the tracks of North London in the gloomy evening light with an indefinite journey time ahead. I put my earphone back in, slumped against the side of the carriage and let the driving beat lull me into a music-induced stupor. This is all too often the reality of commuting by train.

Not that I would really know of course, because my regular commute was by car. This train journey was a relatively unusual escapade into the big city; a rare but welcome variation from my regular commuter surroundings of being cooped up in my little hatchback as I trundled along the b-roads to work in London's anonymous northern suburbs. It wasn't glamorous, but aside from the missing hubcap, the random rear wiper activations and the occasional morning ultimatum whereby I had to choose between a working stereo or a working starter motor, I got by. One thing that had impressed me about this rare venture on to the rail network however, was that I'd been given a substantial discount: a third off my ticket. And the reason for this? No, surprisingly it *wasn't* because of my rugged, commuter charm or stylish shirt and trouser combination, and nor was it because the rail company had recognised the fact that I was sacrificing a journey in such a fantastic set of wheels to be on this miserable train journey. It was in fact merely because I was under the age of 26. Who would have thought it?

After turning 13 I no longer qualified for a cheaper haircut. My half-fare bus pass abandoned me at 14. The masses of 10 per cent discounts made available by my student card deserted me at 21. My Lego club membership expired years ago, and I'm pretty sure I'm no longer eligible for a Blue Peter badge.

Growing up is tough. As a young child you can often slip past entry barriers for free, embracing the theory that as a small person you don't take up a lot of space and that you don't require large amounts of food and drink. There is also the reasoning that you probably won't get much out of the experience as you'll be far more interested in scribbling on walls with crayons, crying or soiling yourself. I imagine the only real complication comes from unwelcome wanderings, but this can always be controlled through the strategic deployment of dungaree straps. If only they were still in fashion.

As you get a bit older you slip into the 'family ticket' discount zone. Here there are a wealth of savings to greet you at every entry booth or ticket machine you come across. The only drawback being that you will still be trailing around behind your designated 'responsible adult', even if you have now been trusted enough to be let off the dungaree straps.

But once you hit your teens a new selection of cheaper tickets and offers seem to vanish with every passing year, making each event or activity that little bit more costly. This coincides inconveniently with an increased level of freedom, as by now you're looking to venture out and explore more of the world, and by the time you're ready to completely break free from the constraints of full-time education (and you're cursing your luck that the children of today are no longer constricted by the now fashion faux-pas of dungarees) any age-based discounts and offers have all but vanished. There's no more cheap meals out, no more student membership at the gym, no more discount drinks in bars and clubs, no more cheap access to canal museums (well, some hurt more than others) and no more smiley-faced stickers to show everyone that *you* paid *less*. It's over. Sure, you can keep on pretending that you're 12 years old, but one day they'll realise that you've grown a beard and they'll charge you the extra £2.50 for a haircut. Trust me.

Before you completely despair, though, there is one area left for you to exploit to your financial benefit; one opportunity to combine that adult-inspired freedom with youthful pricing: train travel! Up until the age of 26 you can literally ride the train of youth and purchase a one-year railcard that offers you a third-off regular train fares across the wonderful British rail network. You can head for the nearest station, throw caution to the wind and jump on board the first train that stops at the platform! You can sneak a window seat, sit back and watch the world whiz—

'Please be aware that due to signal problems on the line, there will be delays to this service'.

Ah, yes that can somewhat ruin it a bit, can't it?

But there is another element to this reduced fare opportunity that offers *even more* potential. This discount isn't just limited to domestic travel. There is a pass available that lets you on to trains abroad; a pass that allows you to venture beyond the disruptive, congested commuter routes of Britain. There is a pass that lets you loose on the expansive, slick, high speed tracks of Europe – the InterRail pass!

I'd vaguely heard of the InterRail pass before, but it was on a recent weekend getaway that my attention was really drawn to its potential. I'd capitalised on a bank holiday weekend by flying out to Zurich in Switzerland, where I boarded a train that took me to the tiny, secluded nation of Liechtenstein. The flights had been fantastically cheap, but I hadn't considered the financial dent that the return train ticket would make into my tight budgeting. One evening I got chatting to a group of English girls in my hostel on the outskirts of Liechtenstein's equally tiny capital, Vaduz. They were making use of a bit of free time after a year-long teaching placement in France and were in the middle of a two week trip around Western Europe by train. The vast inter-country distances they were covering with their relatively inexpensive rail pass (thanks to having purchased significantly discounted 'under 26' tickets) put my hefty standard return fare across not-even-half of Switzerland into perspective. The variety of destinations that they had visited using their passes and the ease at which they went about travelling had intrigued me greatly. The idea of being let loose on the European rail network was very alluring.

Whilst flying to Zurich had been very cheap compared to the cost of the train to Liechtenstein, the delivery method had been far more exciting with the latter. Both journeys had been of a similar length, but with the flight I had been cluelessly transported in an aluminium tube, void of all sense of direction and location. In

14

contrast, on the train journey I'd eagerly watched the changing landscape whiz by the window; from shooting alongside the glistening waters of Lake Zurich and through the quaint little towns that sprung up on its shores, to carving through the mountains with their healthy dousing of snow on top. On the train I had felt far more of a connection between where I had come from and where I arrived at. This is something that air travel denies you, and instead you are stuck crunched up with minimal leg room and often submitted to endless add-on fees, advertisements and miserable queues. Suddenly the realisation that there is hundreds of miles of track running off in all directions; spanning countryside, cutting across borders, running along rivers and delivering you to the heart of some of the most interesting cities in the world suddenly got me very excited: a whole host of languages, cultures and scenery in surprisingly close proximity, and most importantly all linked together by railway lines that are made accessible by the InterRail pass. The thought of swapping being wedged into the armpit of sweaty city workers as I stood crammed into an aging carriage as it lurched around the grubby suburban London landscape on a grim evening for a slick, high-speed adventure on the vast rail-routes of Europe was just too great to ignore.

Unfortunately it's not as simple as that. The problem with gallivanting off into Europe is that it does require *some* money, however cost-effective the ticket may be. To obtain that money, you generally have to work, and to work you normally have to *show up* for work, which often limits any time and opportunity for the afore mentioned Euro-gallivanting. I was also up against it time-wise, as I had just a few months left before I turned 26, and I would therefore soon no longer be eligible for the discounted pass. It certainly was a predicament.

Chapter 2

Hertfordshire to London

I'd spent nearly a year and a half driving to and from work in my severely underpowered hatchback. I was growing weary, as apparently was my car. It had developed some nasty juddering, and I feared it was getting close to packing up altogether. Whenever I stopped at traffic lights I would be subjected to vibrations of such ferocity that my head would bump against the car roof and I used to get strange looks in the rear-view mirror from the driver of the car in front. Perhaps it was payback for all the months of parking it in a dodgy alleyway behind the building where I worked. On one occasion I had been blocked into one of the makeshift parking spaces and I'd had to initiate a 37-point turn to drive free. This intense back and forth movement had been a real test for the clutch (and the muscles in my left leg), and I suspected this juddering was the gearbox telling me that it was time to move on - but how could I escape? How could I end this cycle of tedious traffic jams, engine unreliability and 37-point turns?

Well, it was simple really: I saw a job advert for an exciting position based in the heart of London, I applied for it, and two weeks later I was handing in my notice. It all happened very quickly, and after firing off a few emails to my current and future employers I had soon arranged respective leaving and start dates, and excitingly, there was a gap between them; a gap that would come not long before I turned 26 and lost that final age-based discount.

I sensed an opportunity; a flicker of hope for one final youthful adventure before I ditched the suburban work surroundings for full-blown city employment. Soon I would be spending all of my weekday mornings and evenings squashed on to rush hour train services, relinquishing my travel-autonomy and leaving myself at the mercy of the rail network. Train journeys risked becoming part of a routine that had the negative connotations I'd briefly experienced during rush hour, and so while train travel still held some degree of novelty and excitement it seemed like the perfect opportunity to see what my rapidly diminishing youthful status could allow me to discover on European railways.

It would be fair to say that it hadn't been the most carefully considered of decisions I'd ever made. When you're given the opportunity for adventure – a small window to fill with whatever travel-based exploits you can realistically afford – you don't usually rush off and buy a ticket to Belgium, but this is exactly what I had done.

My plan had been simple: get to the continent, purchase an InterRail pass, and then go wherever the trains would take me. Now obviously it made sense to begin the journey as I meant to go on, which meant taking the train, which of course meant travelling by *Eurostar*. Based upon this you may have thought that Paris would have been the obvious choice of destination to head to first. Well, quite frankly, you're right. Belgium isn't renowned as a glamorous destination. It isn't a country that screams of vibrant culture, dramatic scenery or A-list activity. In fact it is, dare I say it, often perceived as a little…well, dull. Although they do apparently make a good waffle. And let's not forget that Brussels is also more or less the home of the European Union, because barely a month will pass without there being a news report on television featuring a smartly attired broadcast journalist standing outside of a large glass office building and talking about labour migration or European trade policies. And where is that slick, illustrious background location? That's right, Brussels! Or maybe Strasbourg in France. Or possibly Luxembourg.

Belgium is undoubtedly a country of significance, but it still probably wouldn't top many peoples' lists of places to visit before you die, but this didn't matter, because the reason I had chosen Brussels over Paris was because it was cheaper. Late bookings to escape the country in the height of summer rarely come at favourable rates, and having sorted my work leaving date I had conducted a quick internet search to see what was available. Paris was unsurprisingly the most expensive, so I quickly dismissed it. Disneyland didn't quite fit with the style of trip I had in mind and the weekly service to Avignon was fully booked. So Brussels it was. The booking had come with a nice surprise, though: *Eurostar* offered a discounted fare for under-26s. This was very appropriate, and the saving much appreciated as InterRail passes are not valid in your country of origin, so I had to fund this journey separately.

When I told work colleagues where I would be whizzing off to a mere matter of hours after leaving the office for the last time, they were a little puzzled. In fact the response from everyone I mentioned my impending trip to could be summed up quite simply; 'Erm...why Belgium?'

What *did* make my booking to this hub of Euro-political discussion that little bit more exciting however, was that I had booked a one-way ticket, and we all know that there's something adventurous and even a little reckless about booking a one-way ticket. It suggests that you are edgy, and that you like to throw caution to the wind. It also suggests that you embrace freedom and have no restrictions! Even if the truth was that I had a *massive* restriction: I had to be back to start my new job. But what happened between finishing my current job and commencing my new position was an exciting unknown, and that excitement would begin in Belgium! Well, hopefully. There was actually another reason why I had chosen Brussels as my first stop, too.

Back in the mid 90s (when I was happily riding along on all the wondrous discounts of childhood) my dad had been carrying out some work in the transport sector. One afternoon he was given an opportunity to be a guinea pig. Not in any medical lip-stick-on-hamsters sort of a way, but he was actually offered two free tickets aboard a test run of a new special train that they were calling *Eurostar*: a special train that went *under the sea* - to France! He, unsurprisingly, said yes, and very kindly offered not to take me on this free trip to Paris. He did however take my brother with him, which I suppose is only fair as he is older. Unfortunately for them though, the train broke down in the tunnel under the sea, which resulted in them eventually arriving in Paris a lot later than expected and so they only got a very short amount of time in the French capital. Fortunately for *me*, though, some very senior figures in British transport were also on the train, and so as way of an apology everyone on board was given two more free tickets on another test service, but this time to Brussels in Belgium! And guess who got to go this time? That's right - the second choice son for the second choice destination.

Okay, so maybe that's a little harsh. I appreciate the difficulties in choosing between children, but even at that age I was aware that Paris was the city to visit on the continent, and Brussels, well...wasn't. But this didn't lessen my enthusiasm for the trip, because after all, I was going on a train under the sea! I imagined brightly coloured fish swimming past the train windows as we glided through the crystal clear waters of the Channel. Shipwrecks would adorn the seabed beside the tracks, and divers would take breaks from their exciting deep-sea explorations to wave at us in the carriages. Yes, this was going to be great, because I was seven years old, and I was an idiot.

The reality of course was that we ambled along through the Kent countryside before disappearing into a dark tunnel for half an hour, which if I'm being honest was a little boring and contrary to my wild preconceptions of what a train journey under the sea would be like. Still, things got a little better having arrived at Brussels Midi station, because I got to go into the cab of the train, which is something I suspect wouldn't be allowed in current climates. Beyond this exciting and unexpected activity, though, the rest of the trip was pretty unmemorable. In fact all I really remember from the day is sitting in the main square as I wrote a postcard (yes I know, but this was the 90s), spending an age looking for a post box to post the postcard into, seeing a statue of a small urinating boy, giving up looking for a post box and buying a keyring with the Belgium flag on one side and a picture of the small urinating boy on the other. I then remember getting home and immediately throwing up. Not your classic weekend getaway I'm sure you'd agree, but what I hadn't really appreciated at the time was just what a significant moment this train journey symbolised: the connecting of Britain with mainland Europe. It was a massive international achievement, and a great feat of engineering ingenuity that culminated in a physical tie uniting our island with the continent. An eight-years in-the-making project that produced a landmark service that brought down the time and cost of travelling abroad. This was *huge*. But then I was only seven, and I had just inexplicably bought a keyring with a small urinating boy on it.

A little older, and hopefully a little wiser, it now seemed appropriate that I should begin my train adventure across Europe aboard the same service that I had been a test passenger on over 18 years ago. I also felt that I had got off on the wrong foot with Brussels, so I thought I would give it the opportunity to redeem itself.

Chapter 3

London to Brussels

It was an odd last day at work. My line manager forgot about needing to hold an exit interview with me, so it was hastily arranged over lunchtime. This wouldn't have been too much of a problem had it not meant that I missed the vast majority of my leaving lunch, so as my colleagues lazed about in the pub, laughing and joking in between stuffing their faces with delicious Thai food that had been lovingly hand-cooked by a family of native north-Londoners, I was in a hot, stuffy meeting room talking about the effectiveness of brand messaging policies and incentive schemes. All of which seemed a little pointless now, but I stuck it out, and I eventually escaped down to the pub in time to chew on a couple of noodles and down half a lemonade before we had to get back to the office.

The jollities continued after work as my colleagues gathered in a pub in Camden for celebratory drinks. I once again missed a substantial part of this because I had to take my car home before catching a train (that was inevitably delayed) to meet them. Once I finally arrived we had a nice evening sipping beverages in the noisy and crowded surrounds of one of London's most popular nightspots. By midnight I was starting to tire, though. No doubt the exhaustions of a strenuous exit interview, speed-eating Thai food and swapping modes of transport all evening were taking their toll, and so I bid my farewells and slipped off into the night. After all, I had an early start the next day.

It was 5.20 in the morning and I was propped up against the window of the train heading for Euston. It was less than five hours since I had been on this train going in the opposite direction, and the minimal sleep that I'd managed to get in the meantime had not left me feeling overly refreshed. I was excited though, with thoughts of my impending adventure occupying the parts of my brain that were conscious enough to handle it. I had a night's accommodation booked in Brussels, but after that I was free to head off in any direction my imagination (or at least the rail network) allowed.

Emerging out of the station into light morning rain, I made my way down Euston road. The sun was doing its best to break through the clouds, briefly casting a few stray beams of reddened light on the spires of the St Pancras' Renaissance Hotel. Beneath this recently renovated extravagance (the likes of which I would sadly not be residing in during this trip) I slipped into the network of corridors and hallways that link up the various sections of St Pancras station. Here I found a bustling scene of activity that was in stark contrast to the relatively empty streets outside, with throngs of would-be tourists already busy causing havoc with their ridiculously oversized suitcases. The main concourse at St Pancras is often a bit of a gauntlet, although it's still nothing compared to an airport departure lounge. Having said this, I still had my foot run-over twice by stray suitcase wheels on the short walk to the departure hall, although one of these was because I had stopped abruptly when I noticed a piano stood next to one of the escalators. It was bright pink and had a sign on it inviting people to play it. It was a nice feature, but sadly there was no time for early morning serenades today, because I had a train to catch.

I joined a short queue at the international gate having withdrawn my booking print-out slip from my bag. A couple bundled awkwardly through the electronic gates with their hefty luggage in tow, while a slim, suited woman glided through behind almost seamlessly. The man in front of me held the barcode of his e-ticket over the scanner but nothing happened. The red laser beams fluttered around the page but didn't register. After a few seconds of frantic paper-swiping it eventually beeped and allowed him through. There was a small backlog of people beyond the barrier, so I decided to be a good passenger and wait patiently for more space to become available before I stepped up to scan my ticket. Within a couple of seconds, however, a smartly dressed woman had appeared beside me and quickly snatched my piece of paper.

'Follow me!' she barked, strutting off towards a little booth to the side.

What was she doing? I was being a good, conscientious traveller! I was easing the queues! I was *helping*!

It was clearly too late to protest, though, because she had disappeared into the booth. I assumed this was my cue to follow, so I quietly trailed off after her like a naughty schoolboy. She scanned my ticket in her special little room and then let me have it back with a look that suggested she thought I was an idiot. I sighed, took my ticket and moved on. A quick scan of my small bag and a fleeting glance at my passport and I was through to the waiting area. I barely had time to sit down to re-tie a rogue shoelace before an announcement came over the p.a. signalling we could now head to the platform. From entering the station to boarding time it had taken a grand total of nine minutes. None of this two-and-a-half-hours-before-departure business that you get with air travel, and I could have cut it even finer if I'd fancied being a little more reckless. But perhaps my time-efficient cockiness was slightly misplaced, as I hadn't factored in where along the train I needed to be. As I was being slowly drawn up the steeply sloping travelator towards platform 10, I checked my ticket and discovered that my seat was in coach 17. Upon arrival at train level I checked the number of the coach next to me: coach 6. I had some walking to do.

St Pancras station boasts Europe's longest champagne bar, stretching along the upper floor beneath the Grade 1 listed arched roof. The dramatic Victorian architecture is quite a spectacle, and thankfully you don't have to splash out on one of the 17 'styles' of champagne to appreciate it. In any case, I had a bottle of tap water in my bag so I was all set if I got thirsty. As I made my way along the platform I diverted my gaze from the impressive roof to train level, because I was getting dizzy and risked bumping into a pillar. I noticed that apart from the new location (my first *Eurostar* journey had been from its original London home of Waterloo station) little had changed from what I remembered of the train I boarded to Brussels 18 years previously. The carriages were the same white and blue with sweeping yellow trim, but they now looked faded and quite grubby, as well as a little dated, despite the revamped logo on the doors. These days *Eurostar* is more of a familiar travel option for many after nearly two decades of operation, but from looking around at other passengers it can still offer a novel and exciting beginning to a weekend break. This can of course be enhanced by a pre-trip glass of champagne; helping to kick-start the weekend spirit, or at least brighten up the long walk if like me you are destined to be sat at the far end of the train.

Carriage 17 was almost entirely empty. Almost, except for a couple of seats at the far end, one of which was mine. A man in his early 30s (that's right, *he* wouldn't have got the under-26 discount) was sat looking slightly guilty by the window. I stood towering above him, glaring down with my ticket that was clearly displaying my seat number waving gently beside me; the seat that I had *specifically* chosen during my rushed booking. Or at least the seat that I was randomly assigned and couldn't be bothered to change. But still, this guy was taking liberties.

'Oh, er, er, is this your seat?' he mumbled, stumbling over his words.

Of course it bloody is you brainless moron!

'Yes. It. Is.' I replied through gritted teeth, 'But don't worry,' I smiled sarcastically, 'I'll just sit in another seat until *that* one is taken.'

I backed off and dropped down into a seat a couple of rows in front.

I know this wasn't a major hassle for me, but why he couldn't have just sat in his own seat and saved the further disruption of someone finding me in their seat I just couldn't understand. Ironically this is one problem that you don't usually experience on aeroplanes.

Once I had got comfortable in the grey fabric seat, a youngish man with who I assumed was his mother shuffled along the carriage and took two seats on the other side of the aisle from me. She pulled out a small cushion and handed it to him.

'In case you fall asleep' she announced matter-of-factly, much to his embarrassment.

He snatched it off her and stuffed it into the floor space underneath him before shrinking down into his seat and burying his head in a magazine.

We departed from St Pancras International on time, and soon we were powering through the Kent countryside as light rain continued to flick against the window. As it turned out the carriage was less than half full, and so I remained in the rogue seat. The quiet surroundings and smooth action along the rails were very conducive to losing consciousness, and once we hit the blackness of the tunnel there was very little to stop my sleep-deprived body from shutting down for half an hour.

I was brought out of my intermittent slumber by a sharp flash of daylight. We had arrived in France! The grey clouds and drizzle of England had been replaced by bright sunshine and clear skies on the continent. It then wasn't long before we arrived at Lille-Europe station. Why they feel the need to highlight the continent that Lille is in is beyond me, and even with this extra geographical annotation no one appeared keen on getting off the train, so on we pressed across the France-Belgium border. The countryside then started to give way to industrial areas and suburban developments before the train started to slow down as we pulled into Brussels Midi station. Just over two hours is all it had taken, and partly thanks to sustained periods of unconsciousness it barely felt like half of that. It's also worth noting that at no point in the journey had I been required to take off my belt, been pestered to buy a scratchcard or told where to hire the car I didn't need from. I picked up my backpack and headed for the door. The Euro-train adventure had begun!

Chapter 4

Brussels, Belgium

The station was crowded with people rushing off in all directions, suitcases trailing precariously behind them. I made a swift escape out into the sunshine and onto Esplanade de l'Europe. It seemed like a fitting name as I stepped out to begin my trip of trans-European discovery. Despite the lack of sleep I was excited about being outside and I was ready to explore. I tracked down my hostel along Boulevard Emile Jacqmainlaan, and although it was too early to check-in, I dropped off my bag and set off for the centre, heading for where most visits to this city probably begin: Grand-Place de Bruxelles.

The Grote Markt (to be balanced and reference both its French and Flemish names) is a Unesco World Heritage Site, and on this warm, sunny mid-summer Saturday it was packed full of snap-happy tourists. The square is bordered on all sides by a fantastic array of gothic and baroque architecture, with the intricate and ornate facia of the town hall drawing the vast majority of eyes and camera lenses towards it. Not wanting to stand out I too drew out my camera ready to join the masses, but as I did this a Japanese man approached me, smiling slightly manically and waving his own camera in my face.

'Can you take my photo, please!' he said, excitedly.

'Yes, no problem' I replied, stuffing my own camera back into my pocket.

'Great!' He strode purposefully at me. 'You press this button!'

'Yes, thanks' I said, hugely grateful he had taken the time to explain to me how to use a camera.

I took a photo of the man standing in front of the town hall, whilst he continued to smile manically.

'Thanks!' he shouted, grabbing back the camera and scurrying off to admire another set of arches on the other side of the square.

I slipped out my camera and lined it up.

'Excuse me! You take photo of me?'

German was my guess. A young, slender, bespectacled lady with a small flowery suitcase appeared beside me as I lowered my lens.

'Sure' I replied, sighing as I awkwardly jammed my camera back into my jeans.

She struck an almost regal pose, holding her hands together in front of her and adopting a spectacularly emotionless facial expression.

'Thank you' she said matter-of-factly, having been successfully photographed beneath a large, fluttering Belgium flag.

I once again pulled out my camera, and pointed the lens towards the spire above me.

'Hey there! Can you grab a photo of us?'

For *goodness sake*!

Americans. Two of them. Both massive, with the male contingent parading in front of me in an outrageously bright shirt. A shirt that was not buttoned up as high as I would have liked.

I took a deep breath. 'Yes' I retorted sharply, making a clear point of the effort it required to squeeze my camera back into my pocket.

'Great! You gotta press the shutter here' he instructed, pointing at the large button that was on top of the camera - where these buttons *always* are on *every* camera that has *ever* been made.

He then stepped back to join his eager, profusely sweating wife, and together they lined up arm in arm whilst their collective mass comfortably blocked out the picturesque scene behind them. I took the picture, thrust the camera back into the flailing hands of the man and moved swiftly off into the shadows cast by the town hall. I hoped here I would be less visible to tourists desperate to be photographed, because I was fed up of being designated photographer. This saga had bluntly demonstrated one of the pitfalls of solo travelling. It must have been my good-natured face. I made a mental note to scowl in popular locations from now on.

Having given up on trying to photograph the square I headed for a narrow street that led off it. As I did so, a huge wedding party emerged from the entrance of the Town Hall. Weirdly, all the tourists in the square seemed to decide that they would take pictures of the wedding guests. I found this a strange occurrence. Imagine sitting around with friends as they show you their holiday snaps and those crop up.

'Oh that's beautiful! You didn't mention you were out there for a wedding!'

'I wasn't. I just happened to be in the square as they came out and I like photographing strangers with wacky hair attachments.'

'Oh…'

I swiftly moved off into the shadows before I got caught having to take photographs of strangers with wedding guests they didn't know.

As you may expect from a place of such tourist appeal, these side streets are populated with countless shops selling goods aimed at the visitor market. Window displays were packed full of trinkets and knick-knacks, many coated in the black, yellow and red of the national flag, all horribly over-priced and with little charm. This is of course not helped by the fact that many of them also portray that other infamous icon of Brussels: the small urinating boy. I stepped into one of the less congested doorways to have a quick glance to see if the keyring I'd bought 18 years ago was still available. To my not-so-great surprise, it wasn't. I suppose it's good to know that the keyring industry has progressed over the last two decades, as now keyrings seem to have rotating metal centres or double up as bottle openers. One fine specimen even featured the aforementioned urinating child complete with inappropriate sound effect. The world of gimmicky tourist crap endlessly proves itself to be one of great innovation, and I salute it for that.

Back outside I continued to weave through the pedestrian traffic. The good weather had brought out visitors in their droves, and it was no coincidence that many were bustling along this particular street. Around 200 metres south-west of the Grand Place, along Rue de l'Etuve, I came to a small intersection, where I found it; the source of a disproportionately high amount of Brussels' tourist paraphernalia: the *Manneken Pis*. A break in the tightly packed crowd on the street corner revealed this bizarre attraction in all its crotch-streaming glory. The small, 61-centimetre tall bronze statue was made in 1619, and on this hot sunny day he was sporting a very smart red jacket with gold buttons over a white shirt. But regardless of how they dress it up, it's still just a small boy peeing wildly from a stone plinth.

There are numerous 'legends' as to how this statue came about, and perhaps unsurprisingly they all involve a small boy saving the day through wild urination. One says he urinated on enemy troops from a tree having been put up there in a basket for good luck. These enemy troops then apparently went on to lose the battle. Another says he urinated on a fuse that was connected to explosives, which in turn saved Brussels from blowing up. Personally I think local historians are just doing their best to justify a pretty disappointing feature in a dark corner of Brussels. Either that or they're just taking the piss. Talking of which, I noticed one fine specimen of a tourist recreating the classic 'waterfall' photo pose, where you lean back with your mouth open so it looks like the water is going into your mouth. When done by waterfalls it looks tacky, but in *this* context it raises some quite serious questions about the perpetrator. All in all it was as disappointing as I remember from my first visit, even if they had bothered to clothe it this time, although really, how dignified can it ever be? The anti-climax is further enhanced when you discover that this isn't even the real statue. Since 1965 a replica has stood on the plinth as apparently people kept nicking it (god knows why) and so the original is hidden away within the Maison du Roi in the Grand Place.

Thankfully my attention was drawn away from these disturbing scenes by an entrance way in the wall to my left. A sign beside the opening read; 'Waffles 1 Euro'. I checked my watch. It was twenty past twelve, which I'm reasonably confident is an acceptable time to eat waffles. I then checked my wallet and found a loose one Euro coin. It was all coming together nicely. I stepped inside. To call it a shop would be overstating things a little. You'll be aware of a retail outlet – well this was a retail *in*let; a waffle crevice if you will, although that probably doesn't sound as alluring. Inside this gap in the wall was a hatchway with a small lady in a hat standing behind it.

'Can I help you?' she said quite angrily, which was a little surprising given that I appeared to be her only business.

'Oui! Je voudrais une waffle, s'il vous plaît!'

Yes, I was very proud of my excellent French.

'Which one?' she persisted in English.

I don't know, some people just don't make the effort to speak the local language.

I hadn't realised there would be a choice, I just wanted a *normal* waffle. I quickly scanned the shelf inside the little hatch and noticed a pan containing a viscous brown liquid.

'Erm...avec...chocolate, s'il vous plaît!'

Belgium is meant to be good at chocolate, so this choice made sense. I was being clever and local. I was also still trying my best to both speak French and be cheerful. She was doing neither.

'One Euro eighty' she said flatly, having grabbed a waffle from a grill in a wholly unenticing manner and slopped a ladle of chocolate sauce over it.

I stood there perplexed for a moment while she stared at me expectantly. One Euro eighty seemed very expensive for a one Euro waffle. I glanced down at the one euro coin I had ready in my hand. The lady emitted an impatient sigh. I scowled at her, then reached into my pocket to retrieve a five Euro note and grudgingly handed it to her. Why had the price gone up 80 per cent in the time I had taken to step inside this waffle hole? Unfortunately my French doesn't extend to 'what the hell do you mean "one Euro eighty"? It says *one Euro* on your bloody sign!' so I had to settle for a resentful 'merci' as she handed me my change.

Distracted by the sudden rise in inflation that had apparently gripped the waffle industry, I hadn't noticed what else I'd been given. Haphazardly stuck into the dripping waffle was a tiny plastic fork. Now back outside I assessed it carefully. Here I had a waffle on a small polystyrene tray, coated in masses of dark, runny chocolate, and with a tiny plastic fork protruding from it. The tiny plastic fork was already practically drowned in the chocolate sauce. Belgium was really testing my patience now. How the hell was I supposed to eat this? I then looked down again and realised something even worse: I was wearing a crisp, new, plain *white* t-shirt. Brilliant. This was going to be a chocolate disaster. I started jabbing tentatively at the waffle with the fork. The sea of chocolate masked what lay beneath, and as I prodded around the fork got stuck in the polystyrene, snapping the end off the already short handle. The now broken fork had also split the polystyrene container. I let out a deep sigh and backed cautiously into a nearby alleyway. I had to get well away from the crowd of ridiculous tourists that risked callously bumping into me and causing me to spill chocolate all over myself. I was backpacking and so I couldn't afford to get covered in chocolate stains so early into my trip when I had such a limited supply of spare clothing.

I slowly made my way along a collection of empty back roads as I picked away with the remaining bit of fork, trying desperately to break apart the waffle segments into eatable chunks whilst protecting my pristine attire. So far Belgium was not redeeming itself at all: I had been bombarded by photography requests, I had fought crowds to see a rubbish statue, I had been ripped off for a waffle and now I was on the cusp of creating a terrible confectionary-based mess. I was not impressed, but thankfully, after 10 minutes of frantic mashing with the remainder of the plastic fork I had broken the waffle down into eatable chunks. I then carefully scooped them into my mouth, leaning over to shield my t-shirt from any stray blobs of chocolate. Despite the administrative hassles of this whole process, the waffle was very tasty. I hadn't realised quite how hungry I was, having not eaten since leaving home over seven hours ago. The rich chocolate also gave me an energy boost that after the disappointment of my visit so far was much needed.

Cheered up by my mid-day indulgence and slightly amazed that I had survived the ordeal without decorating my t-shirt, I pressed on towards my next stop. I didn't know a lot about what I was going to see, or even where it was, but my sketchy knowledge of its existence was enough to get me striding purposefully along

Anspachlaan before ducking down into De Brouckere metro station. In the large underground area I found a map of the various available routes. Paris gets some stick for having a complicated underground train system, but on this evidence Brussels was keen to compete in that area too. De Brouckere appeared to be at the centre of the network, with a series of colourful lines heading north and south. There were also lines heading west and east, which then sprouted off in other directions. One of these lines then headed a little north and then back west again, but also south and west. There were some mini crossover lines that went in other directions as well. All of the lines were helpfully colour coded, including a dark red line, a yellow line, and a slightly-less-yellow yellow line. There were also two lines that were similar shades of green. Thankfully they were also numbered; there was a 2, a 90, a 23, a 1B and a 56 amongst others. Did I mention that many of the stations also had both French and Flemish names? It was all a little confusing. Luckily there was a station in the far top left corner that had a little symbol next to it that looked like it related to the place I was heading for, so all I had to do now was work out how to get there. It looked like heading west was the first stage, so I headed over to the ticket machines. At the third machine I tried I finally got issued a ticket, which I then swiped through one of the electronic gates that allowed me through to get down to the platform.

The first journey proved to be simple. I boarded a train that arrived within seconds of me getting to the platform, and then I travelled four stops west (and then slightly south) to Beekkant, which conveniently didn't appear to have a duel language name. I then switched platforms to catch a 1B train north. At the second stop the train seemed to empty, with only a couple of people remaining in the carriage. There was then an announcement that was barely coherent thanks to the poor quality speakers, let alone the tricky language combination. It was enough to trigger the remaining passengers to slowly rise, though, and with bemused looks on their faces they got off the train. I sensed I should follow, so I got up and left too. I was at Simonis station, which was a junction between the yellow and the slightly-less-yellow yellow lines. Unhelpfully the map on the platform was arranged differently so it could be accommodated within a horizontal sign. The digital board hanging above the platform was also selective about which language it used for stations, which all left me a little confused. After letting a couple of trains go past I eventually got bored of hanging around in the hot underground station and so I boarded the next train. I fixed my eyes on the map as we pulled up at the next stop, and thankfully I was on course. A few minutes later we arrived at Heysel/Heizel. It had taken all of the chocolate waffle energy I had acquired to get there, but finally, after surfacing in a north-western suburb of the Belgian capital I saw the sign; I had arrived at Expo 58!

Okay, I was 54 years late, and for that I can't *entirely* blame the Brussels metro, but the site of the *Exposition Universelle et Internationale de Bruxelles*, also known as the *Brusselse Wereldtentoonstelling*, or *Brussels World's Fair* still has some significant visitor draws, the main one of these being the event's centre piece: the *Atomium*. Standing at 102 metres in height, this impressive and eye-catching sight is a representation of the molecular structure of an iron crystal cell, handily magnified 165 billion times. On this sunny day, the nine spheres - or 'atoms' - were glistening in the sun, immediately putting the small urinating child in a dark corner into perspective. I stood for a few moments at the end of the grass-centred promenade that leads up to it, with the slightly jaded looking Centenary Palace behind me, admiring its striking form. Beneath the giant reflective atoms was the visitor centre, and after a short queue I purchased a 'combo' ticket. This gave me access to the *Atomium* and the neighbouring *Mini Europe*, which I had no idea as to what it was, but I like benefiting from economies of scale.

On closer inspection I was impressed at how modern and untarnished the attraction looked given that it was 54 years old. I then discovered from information displayed within the walk-through exhibition that leads you up, down and around the spheres via connection tubes that it had been heavily refurbished between 2004 and 2006. The re-surfaced stainless steel spheres now house temporary exhibitions, with 'Water for All' being the theme during my visit. Once I had ascended the escalator into the first sphere I was greeted by information boards, models, videos and interactive displays that looked at the world's water supplies and how water usage impacts on people and the planet. The surroundings provide an intriguing and novel space to display this information, although without windows you're given very little idea as to where it's being staged. The numbering system can also add to the slightly disorientating effect of the exhibition as you make your way up and across several spheres to level 5, before dropping back down to level 6. It was on one of these levels that I found a statistics board that listed a large number of anecdotal figures relating to the original 1958 event. I scanned through the mass of exorbitantly high numbers; many of which are impressive, but also probably quite unremarkable when considered in context, such as the 70 restaurants that served the complex, the 20,000 staff employed to create the pavilions across the site or the 280 'charming fair hostesses' that looked after visitors. But some of the stats mixed in to the list caught my eye for their slightly perverse nature; apparently 31,000 people fell sick at Expo 58, 5 people died, 27 'hopeless people tried to commit suicide', whilst 2,000 children 'ran lost' at the event. I suppose I respected their honesty, and I also found myself developing an odd appreciation for the slightly off-kilter Belgian sense of humour.

A final escalator through a tube of flashing neon lights returned me to ground level and back outside, which left me once again a little confused. I'd noticed in the visitor booklet that had been given to me alongside my ticket that there was a viewing platform, but I certainly hadn't seen one. I looked back through the windows of the visitor centre and realised that there was a separate queue for a central lift that evidently led directly up the central 'rod' to the top sphere. I re-entered the complex and joined the queue, and a short while later I was taking in the fantastic panoramic views out across the grounds of the exhibition site and beyond towards central Brussels.

Impressed with the Atomium experience I moved on to utilise the rest of my 'combo' ticket and I entered Mini Europe. I should have probably guessed what it was by the name, as inside I found a long weaving pathway that led around miniature re-constructions of European cities. They were very neatly presented, with tiny moving vehicles, people and attractions, but what excited me was the fact that I would hopefully be seeing the full-scale versions of some of these places in the coming days. The idea of Europe being so accessible across a small area as represented by this attraction seemed like a fitting physical metaphor for what the train pass I hoped to buy tomorrow would enable me to do. It was this powerfully philosophical thought, along with three more requests for photographs that made me realise I was getting quite weary, and so I decided that it was probably time I headed back to the city centre to check-in to my hostel.

It was early evening as I pushed through the door to what I thought was my residence for the night. I reclaimed my bag and stood at reception to get my room key. What I hadn't expected was that the key came with a map with a red circle on it. The man on the desk then informed me that my accommodation was actually in a separate block, close to the Grand Place. This was an unexpected development, but with little scope to question it I set off back towards the tourist centre. Twenty minutes later and I was still fighting my way through the evening crowds as I tried to make sense of the poorly photocopied map. I ended up walking through the Grand Place three times before finally finding the tiny alleyway where my hostel block was. Unfortunately this wasn't the end of my struggles, as the electronic key card consistently failed to allow me access through the door. I repeatedly tapped it against the sensor in every conceivable manner (much to the entertainment of a group of young Belgians sat in a nearby doorway) until I eventually got the literal green light to go through. Inside I found a group of travellers sat in deck chairs, apparently oblivious to my struggles on the other side of the door. Five sets of stairs with handrails loosely attached with masking tape guided me up through what appeared to be a building site to my attic room. It was empty of people, but full of bags with clothing spilling out of them. There was also a large water pistol on the floor. This looked ominous, but the stair climb had been the final exertion my body was willing to endure after a long and busy day, and so I ignored the potential impending threat of aqua-warfare, and after dumping my bag I hauled myself up on to the one remaining bunk bed and crashed out.

I was awoken suddenly about half an hour later by the door being thrown open. A group of guys a little older than myself burst into the cramped space, shouting and jumping around. They were French, and as soon as they realised I was there they seemed very embarrassed about their dramatic entrance.

'Ah, pardon!' the lead Frenchman said, clutching his mouth apologetically.

'Ah, c'est non problem!' I replied, trying to sound as French and relaxed about it as I could. They told me that they were in Brussels for the weekend on a stag party. This explained the water pistol. They also said that they would be drinking but would try and be quiet when they got back late. I used my best French - which isn't as French as I'd probably have hoped - to say that it was fine, and that they should enjoy themselves and have a good Christmas. It was at this point that their fourth member crashed into the room. The door was flung open (just missing my leg) to reveal the newly emerged figure, who was inexplicably firing imaginary lasers at me whilst making associated sound effects.

'Bonjour!' I cried out instinctively, which was a little odd really, but then everyone burst out laughing. Although this scene had all the makings of a terrible night's sleep, they all seemed well meaning and polite, and so I was happy enough to set off back down the treacherous staircase to leave my dorm counterparts to their laser battles.

Emerging from the hostel having had a short period of recuperation, I could now appreciate just what a great location it was, with the Town Hall peeking out at the end of the alleyway. I headed into the square and turned left, soon finding myself in a collection of narrow streets that were packed with restaurants, their tables spilling out beneath awnings onto the cobbles and filled with relaxed holiday diners. I found a bar along Grasmarkt and settled down for a bite to eat and a pint of Blanche de Bruges, looking out on the street scene and soaking up the summer evening atmosphere. It had been a busy but successful first day out on the rails, and I was excited about pressing on to see what else I could explore on the tracks of Europe. After a couple of drinks and one last stroll through the softly lit night time surrounds of the Grand Place, I decided that I needed to try and get some proper sleep, so I headed back to the hostel, ready for whatever night time intrusions may await.

Chapter 5

Brussels to Amsterdam

I woke up early the next morning, and after quickly showering and clothing myself I was soon on my way. I'd heard the French collective come in at about two o'clock, but they had tried so hard in their drunken state to be quiet and careful, whispering and shushing each other as they walked into everything (including each other) as they got ready for bed, that I didn't mind. They seemed like classic stag party participants in many ways; heavy drinking, larking about and...well, laser battles I suppose, but they were also oddly conscientious. I liked them. I had a newly positive perception of the French. Talking of new perceptions, having dropped my key card in a box downstairs (thankfully I didn't have to trek back to the other hostel to check out) I entered the Grand Place once more from the alleyway to find it almost completely empty. Never one to waste an opportunity I quickly pulled out my camera and snapped away, free of interruption. Things had certainly picked up in regards to my opinion of Brussels, and in the fresh morning air and sunshine I was in high spirits, so I decided to take an elongated route back towards the station. As I stood on the cobbles in the square, the sound of bells reverberated off the tall buildings that enclosed it. I decided that I would follow the sound, and after five or so minutes I found myself climbing the steps to Cathedrale des Saints Michel-et-Gudule/Kathedraal van Sint-Michiel en Sint-Goedele. Inside a mass was taking place - impressively in four languages. It was very busy with Sunday worshipers, and so after lingering for a few minutes to take in the calm atmosphere that churches offer, I dropped a few coins in the collection box and headed back out. A neat little park sloped down away from the cathedral, and there were people sitting beneath trees, including the peculiar sight of a homeless man reclined on a sun lounger.

To the south I came across Parc de Bruxelles, or Warandepark; home to an unusual art exhibition that featured various seemingly unlinked objects on top of large metal poles. There was a hot air balloon, a partially eaten slab of chocolate and a golden clam among others. The park itself is book-ended by the Federal Parliament building to the north east and the Palais du Roi to the south west. The latter was quickly developing a collection of tourist coaches outside its gate. No doubt their camera-clad passengers were in the near vicinity, so I decided not to hang around, fearing more requests for third-party involvement in the documentation of other people's holidays. Further on I walked through Place Royale - another impressively set cobbled square where a horse-drawn carriage wouldn't have looked out of place. A gold, glinting dome then caught my attention, and this became my next route marker, leading me down the long, straight Regentschapstraat until I arrived outside the partially-scaffolded Palais de Justice de Bruxelles. More appealing than this stone monolith, though, was an impressive viewpoint out across the city. I hadn't noticed much of an incline, but from here you could see right across to the Grand Place and beyond, with the *Atomium* even faintly visible in the distant haze. A glass lift then took me back down to city level, and after meandering through a series of quiet back streets I came out unexpectedly into a flea market. It was packed with traders and perspective buyers, all scanning the piles of what to me looked like junk as they looked for a bargain. There were hoards of brass objects on offer, with candlesticks, door handles, hinges and jewellery all in great supply. There were also tables of ancient electronic goods, including portable radios and stacks of remote controls that I would be very surprised if they actually worked, as well as torn furniture dotted around the edges of the market alongside rusting bicycles and faded lampshades. It really was an intriguing array of disjointed crap.

I eventually found my way out of the maze of informal aisles that had formed between the rows of junk and managed to get back down to the main road. Here another market was taking place, but this one offered the more conventional selection of fresh produce. As a result there was also a more cosmopolitan crowd, which meant a lot of pushing and shoving as I fought my way through the olive-buying fraternity to get to the station. The contrast between how this area had been when I had arrived yesterday to how it was today was remarkable. The seemingly endless lines of stalls had sprung up over night, and would no doubt disappear as quickly at the close of play. I wouldn't be around to see it though, because I had a train to catch.

Back inside Brussels Midi station I found my way to the international ticket office.

'Bonjour, please take a ticket' a man in a suit said at the entrance.

I did as I was told, tearing off a ticket from the adjacent machine and sitting down on a cushioned bench. Once my number was called I stepped up to the desk.

'Bonjour! Can I buy an InterRail ticket, please?

The man behind the desk eyed me suspiciously before replying, 'No. I cannot do that here.'

'Oh.'

This kind of threw a spanner in the works. In fact this had the potential to ruin the whole point of my trip.

'Where are you going?' he quickly continued, clearly noticing my crestfallen expression.

'Amsterdam'

'Okay, well, I think maybe you buy a ticket to Amsterdam, then you get a pass from there. I get you a cheap ticket. You under 26, yes?'

'I am, yes!' I replied, cheered slightly by this confirmation that once again my age was saving me money. After all, this was the whole point of my trip!

He tapped at his computer and soon a giant boarding pass-style ticket was presented to me. I handed over 26 Euros (a fitting sum given my discount-eligible age) and headed back out on to the station concourse.

To celebrate yet another discounted train ticket, I splashed out on a sandwich. I took a seat near a pillar and began unwrapping it. As I did so I became aware of the lady in the seat next of me. She had suddenly started rocking back and forth, and just as I turned back to face my sandwich she started crying. This was very alarming, especially as it was only a ham and lettuce sandwich. I mean, it wasn't as if it was egg and sardines. I looked around, trying to decide the best course of action, when suddenly her wailing turned into manic laughter. This was all too much. I re-wrapped my sandwich, picked up my bag and moved away. I decided it might be better if I ate it on the train.

The platform was more or less deserted, with just a couple of lone people lingering near a drinks machine by the steps that led up from the underground concourse. The train was already sitting by the platform, and so with my unreserved ticket I wandered along towards the front and boarded a carriage. Judging by the departure board the route between Brussels and Amsterdam was a common one, and so it wasn't all that surprising that this early afternoon service was quite empty. I walked about halfway along the aisle before dropping down into one of the large blue seats on the right hand side. I then pulled out my sandwich and began eating it undisturbed. A couple of men got on just after me and took seats on the other side of the aisle. Having noticed me eating, they must have decided that they should do the same, as they quickly got out some bread from their backpacks. They were obviously keen to take it a step further though, as they then pulled out a block of cheese, some cherry tomatoes and even a tin a tuna. This was a full on picnic! They also had a large bottle of lemonade that they carefully poured into small plastic cups. They then set about cutting the cheese with a small knife on the fold down table. You certainly couldn't be doing *that* on an aeroplane. It was an impressive operation, although now the carriage smelt quite strongly of fish.

The train filled up at Antwerp, which included the arrival of a very loud group of people who probably not entirely through choice positioned themselves at opposite ends of the carriage. However they then spent the rest of the journey shouting across at each other in between seemingly unsuccessful attempts at answering the many phone calls they were getting. The shouting and incessant ring tone interruptions did an excellent job of ruining the otherwise calming nature of the journey, and so I tried my best to block them out by wedging my earphones firmly into my ears and turning up the volume.

Our arrival on Dutch soil a short time later felt a little staged. Out of the window a large river emerged beside the tracks flanked by two massive dykes. Along these impressive flood defences were paved cycle lanes filled with families out on weekend excursions. In the distance I then noticed a nicely restored wooden windmill. I raised an eyebrow at no one in particular at the slightly clichéd nature of this display, half expecting a member of the train staff to come down the aisle selling clogs at any moment, but soon the quintessential countryside views gave way to more suburban surrounds, and then it wasn't long before we were rolling up into the Dutch capital.

Chapter 6

Amsterdam, The Netherlands

Amsterdam Centraal was busy. There were people everywhere dragging masses of luggage in conflicting directions. It was all in stark contrast to Brussels Midi station, but then I had expected it to be a bit livelier here, and that was one of the reasons why I'd chosen it as my next stop. Once I had cut through the throngs of people on the main concourse I found my way to the travel centre, as I thought I'd sort out my next train journey whilst I was at the station. A series of poles with red material strips between them indicated a queuing system that I politely obeyed. As before I was then required to take a numbered ticket, although here there was a pleasant lady in a blue uniform on hand to pass it to me, which certainly took the stress out of it. As with the platforms, the travel centre was also very busy. Backpackers lined the limited available seating, with more occupying floor space next to walls or pillars, their rucksacks dumped haphazardly around them to form an obstacle course of straps and brightly coloured fabric. I stepped carefully over the travel-weary bodies and their associated belongings until I found a bit of pillar space for myself. I checked my ticket and assessed its number in relation to that of the digital screen that hung from the ceiling. It confirmed to me that I had a long wait. I dropped my bag down and adopted a casual lean against my chosen pillar. If I was going to stick this out I didn't want to look all hot and flustered as I did so; I wanted to look calm and casual. This worked brilliantly for a while, but then boredom set in as the numbers took an age to increase on the screen. I began cursing under my breath and

48

wondering why on earth it took everyone so long to buy a simple bloody train ticket.

Eventually, after a good 40 minutes (by which point my casualness had deserted me and I'd slumped ungraciously to the floor like everyone else) my number flashed up. I grabbed my bag and hurried over to the desk indicated by the screen.

'Hello, how can I help?'

'Hi, can I have a ticket to Copenhagen for tomorrow night, please.'

The man tapped at his computer. 'Did you want a seat or a bed?'

Who did he think I was, The *Queen*?!

'Just a seat, please' I replied, slowly shaking my head as if this was the silliest question I'd been asked all year.

He tapped a little more before biting his lip.

'I'm sorry, there are no seats left for tomorrow night.'

'Oh.'

This wasn't good. I had a cleverly devised plan and this wasn't part of it. 'What about…a bed?' I hesitantly enquired, because having the luxury of a bed was unlikely to fit in with my budget travel plans.

He looked back at his screen and screwed up his eyes. 'I'm afraid there are no beds available, either.'

'Oh.' I said once again.

'You can travel the following night?'

This was no good. I had places to be and I couldn't afford to spend an extra night here if my schedule was going to work. Amsterdam also books up quickly in summer and it would have been unlikely I would have found accommodation for another night at such short notice.

'Or you can travel during the day tomorrow?' he continued, evidently sensing my anguish at the implications of not getting the ticket I'd hoped for.

'Okay, how much is that?'

'Well,' he did some more tapping, 'a single ticket…to Copenhagen,' his speech slowed as he played for time whilst the computer caught up with his tapping demands, 'changing *twice*,' as if this helped justify the extra processing time on behalf of the computer, 'is…' a final finger-flourish over the enter key, '…one hundred and eighty-five Euros!' he announced triumphantly.

Shit. That didn't fit in with my budget plans either. I stood in silence for a few seconds.

'Are you going anywhere after Copenhagen?' he asked softly. I think he felt bad for being so triumphant in his delivery of the shocking price information. 'Because it would be cheaper to get an InterRail pass.'

Yes! I shouted in my head.

'Yes!' I shouted at the man, half a second later. He looked a little taken aback. 'And I can buy that…here?' I asked, pointing at the desk to add unnecessary clarity. After the incident in Brussels I was under the impression that you could only buy these passes online or from selected outlets.

'Yes, no problem!'

'Brilliant!'

Now we were both happy. Admittedly I would lose time in Amsterdam, but the earlier connection would save me a lot of money and put my time schedule back – quite literally - on track. He happily tapped away for a few more moments, revealing the price of the under-26 multi-journey pass to be less than what the single journey from Amsterdam to Copenhagen would have cost on its own. This was brilliant. He then disappeared off into a back room after checking my passport. He returned soon after to fill out a few more details and then finally he presented me with my pass. It was another large format ticket but this time it was stapled into a booklet, which he explained to me was where I needed to fill in details of each journey that I made. He then handed me a map of the routes and some seat reservations for my long and slightly complex journey to Copenhagen. Apparently most international services require seat reservations, and for around three Euros each I wasn't going to argue with him. I took my collection of newly acquired ticket-based paraphernalia and strode cheerily out of the travel centre, only pausing slightly when faced with a particularly gangly pair of legs to step over, and again to briefly absorb the irony of how long I had ended up taking at the ticket desk having moaned earlier. But I couldn't waste too much time reflecting on my ticket-buying inefficiencies, because now I was up against it to fit in some interesting activities in this lively city.

Amsterdam has a bit of a reputation. It's not necessarily a bad one, it just occasionally errs on the debauched side. *Liberal* is perhaps the kindest word for it. It is a city renowned for its relaxed and friendly atmosphere. Or for drugs and prostitution if you're being blunt. Yes there are lots of lovely canals and bridges to stroll across, but it's very difficult to avoid the city's more notorious side, especially once the sun goes down. I know this partly through reputation, but also because I had been here once before.

It was the previous summer, and I'd decided to go on an overseas road trip with a group of friends. We had got together and mapped out lots of exciting routes and permutations to make for an unforgettable journey. Unfortunately we then realised that we didn't have a lot of leave to take from our respective work places, and so a lot of the far-flung and exotic destinations were not feasible. As a compromise we ended up driving to a music festival in Luxembourg, which was a lot of fun. To make more of a trip of it though, we had taken a detour on the way, leaving a couple of days early and driving from the outskirts of London to Haarlem on the outskirts of Amsterdam in one day. It was that evening that we all encountered the Dutch capital for the first time.

It had been a very efficient drive, but after 12 hours on the road (and briefly on the ferry) we were pretty drained. We made the 20 minute train journey from Haarlem to Amsterdam Centraal and wandered off in search of something to eat. We found a nice little Italian restaurant and ordered some beers and pizza. The much needed food and cool refreshing beverages were very welcome, and twinned with the warm summer evening air our road trip holiday spirit was quickly restored. Having finished our meal we headed out in search of further refreshment, and before we really knew what was happening we found ourselves in the excessively carpeted and heavily cushioned basement of a bar. Soon we had jugs of beer in front of us and then a large sheisha appeared. We weren't exactly sure where this had come from, but not wanting to lose face in front of the other inhabitants that we could just about make out through the haze, we passed the pipe around. None of us are smokers, and so we weren't very good at it. At first we thought that perhaps there were some 'special' substances in the pipe, but then it was decided that we were actually all just holding our breaths too long, and this combined with the alcohol and the effects of a the long and tiring day on the road was what was leaving us feeling a little light headed.

After dragging ourselves out of the many cushions we moved on to somewhere a little less underground and fabric-lined, and found a small, unassuming bar off a side street. In here we got another drink, and also a muffin to share for desert as all the sheisha puffing had made us a little hungry again. It had struck us as being a little odd that a muffin would come with a warning label on the packaging, but with our slightly blurred vision we had no hope of reading the tiny print. A couple of us chewed at the chocolaty mound before finishing up our drinks and setting off back to the station. It was soon after this that things took a slightly odd turn.

We stumbled along to Dam Square, which turned out to be in the opposite direction to where we wanted to go, but we had become distracted. One of my co-travellers had started giggling like a child for no obvious reason. When he was quizzed over this he just shrugged. I wasn't aware of this slight oddity however, because I was experiencing a far more exciting development: I had suddenly realised that I could see in *seven* directions *simultaneously*! This was fantastic, and as a keen sightseer and visitor to new places it was very handy. Why I hadn't realised I could do this before was a little strange, especially given how beneficial it was now proving as my eyes darted about, taking in the interesting array of buildings that surrounded us, including the impressive 17th Century Royal Palace. Unfortunately this newly discovered skill was overshadowed by an altogether more concerning realisation: everything was *tilted*. The buildings were all at a slight angle, and so were the roads. Again, I couldn't believe I hadn't noticed this earlier in the evening, because it was such a marked problem with the city. The signs were all tilted, the streetlights sticking up in bizarre positions and the trams looked like they could topple over at any moment. In a city that has a large proportion of cobbling it struck me as a bit of an oversight as it made walking conditions even trickier. It was certainly a poor planning decision. Luckily I am an adaptable person, and so I adopted an appropriate counter-lean, that put everything back into the correct perspective. This was a little difficult given the uneven walking surface, but I did my best.

Unfortunately, as we turned right along Mozes en Aaronstraat and began heading in the *right* direction to get back to the station, we passed a couple of people that greatly irritated me. Given the lengths that I was going to as I tried to restore some normality to this strange, slanted world, these two people were walking along as if there *wasn't* a slant! As a result they were at odds with everything around them. They looked *ridiculous*. What annoyed me more was that as I approached them along the narrow pavement they didn't even make an attempt to adjust themselves with a temporary lean so I could get by more easily. The result of this was that I lightly bumped the shoulders of one of the pair. I couldn't believe their rudeness. My giggling friend found all this hilarious, but then he was quickly distracted by the unparalleled comic-value of an empty street bench.

Half an hour later and we were back on the train to Haarlem. The fits of laughter had subsided and thankfully the railway had been built on the flat so I could go back to an upright position. This was good as my side was beginning to ache quite heavily with the strain of leaning. One of my friends then pulled out a label from his pocket. It was the one from the muffin packaging. The *warning* label. It slowly became apparent that it may not have been an ordinary muffin, and that potentially – *potentially* – it could have had some impact on the evening's developments.

So here I was, back in Amsterdam. Thankfully everything seemed structurally in order this time as I cut through an alleyway and into the busy pedestrianised Nieuwendijk where my hostel was located. After experiencing the 'alternative' side of the city on my previous visit, I was determined to sample a more culturally engaging side this time. My plan didn't start well. I checked into the hostel whilst being monitored by a large black cat that sat on the bar-come-reception desk. It kept a watchful eye on me as I filled out my details on the check-in form, and then menacingly licked its paw. The cat menacingly licked its *own* paw, that is. I am not a paw-licker. (And even if I was, I don't think I'd be a menacing one.) I found my room at the end of a long dark corridor, where upon entering I was immediately hit by an overpowering herbal aroma. Clothes and Scandinavians were strewn across the room, whilst thick smoke drifted in through the window that opened out onto the smoking 'garden'. I dumped my bag on the one available bed and headed off out again.

I hadn't ventured beyond the central enclave of Amsterdam in my previous visit, but now I was heading out over the angular rings of the city's canal network that give it its distinctive geographical structure. I went through the largely familiar surrounds of Dom Square, which was a little more upright in appearance than I recalled, before crossing the first of the canal rings on Raadhuisstraat to the west. Modified gondolas and small cruising boats jostled for position along the water's edge as they fought for tourist trade. The masses of bicycles are also one of the more striking features of Amsterdam. Cyclists whiz by at a constant rate along the many dedicated lanes, whilst every post and railing in sight is engulfed in bikes like a thick metallic ivy. I became slightly disorientated by the number of canals I was crossing over, but as I closed in on what I thought was the fourth one, I spotted what I was looking for. It was quite a distinctive building, and not necessarily for its architectural values, but more because of the long, winding queue that was leading up to it. This was Anne Frank's house.

The story of Anne Frank is one of the Second World War's more compelling and noted, especially in its contrast to the many graphic tales of fighting. During the Nazi occupation of the Netherlands the young Anne Frank and her family went into hiding in this building –

her father's office - where she kept a diary that detailed her time cooped up in the small building, hidden from the enemy and the outside world. The diary was subsequently published after the war and has been translated into more than 60 languages. This building has now become a highly symbolic location in regards to the mistreatment of Jews during the war, and the museum that now exists here is unsurprisingly very popular.

I eventually found the end of the queue and took my place in it, intrigued by what I knew of the story and keen to find out more about the setting for the infamous book. I was also hoping to gain some more insight into the city, and a different perspective to that of which I had gotten before.

The queue was slow moving. I hadn't brought anything out with me so I had little to entertain myself with as I waited. This included not bringing a jumper or jacket as it had been warm and sunny when I'd set off. Suddenly though, the clouds moved in and began to dispense some unwelcome rain. In many ways it gave an atmospheric tinge to what we were about to experience, but ultimately I just got very cold and wet. A Norwegian couple behind took pity on me, and began shielding me with one of their umbrellas. This seemed to happen at the expense of their daughter, who was then forced to take shelter under the ledge of the neighbouring building. I then felt guilty, cold and wet. After an hour of queuing I finally made it to the relative warmth and dryness of the museum entrance. I parted with eight Euros (I didn't qualify for any discount here despite my bedraggled student-like appearance) and I headed off into the network of small rooms.

Growing up I would often be dragged around museums (mainly led by my dad), and like many children, unless there were a lot of buttons to press, wheels to turn, lights to light up or any other kind of interactive element to the exhibitions I could distract myself with,

I would find it very difficult to maintain an interest. I think years of persistence has finally worn me down though, and the need to visit a museum has become ingrained in me, almost as a guilt-reflex for all the other (what I might refer to as 'more conventionally fun') activities I could have on a trip or holiday, whether that's messing about in a swimming pool on a Greek island, climbing a mountain in Bulgaria or playing football on a campsite in France. That's not to say I don't enjoy museums or take an interest in learning, I'm just easily distracted by more active experiences. As I've grown up I like to think that I've developed a wider knowledge and enthusiasm for discovering things about the world, though, (that travelling has no doubt enhanced) and I've become far more willing to invest time and energy in paying them more attention.

I was impressed with the *Anne Frank Museum*, and thought it was certainly worth the wait. Narrow, creaking wooden staircases link up dimly lit passages and rooms that each hold stories from the family's time hidden away there. Diary extracts and reconstructed photographs hang on the otherwise bare walls as part of minimalist displays; a few explanatory passages of text give each room a little context, but ultimately it's left to the atmosphere that all these elements draw together in the confined spaces that give the museum its appeal. The restricted space in the building also explained the long queuing times, but its popularity is certainly understandable, and fitting in all the eager visitors is clearly no mean feat. The fact that once you are inside you don't feel crowded by other people is quite remarkable. There were even moments when I was squinting in the limited light to read a diary excerpt on the wall – tricky given the swirly, italicised handwriting - when someone would come in the room behind and almost make me jump. The museum took less than 40 minutes to go around, but I hadn't rushed it or felt under pressure to move around it any quicker. It may seem a little odd to have spent more time waiting to get in than actually being inside, but it was worth it.

I had almost dried out as I pushed myself through the glass door of the exit, where I found the sun had returned. I grabbed a bite to eat and continued to wander around the canals as the light deteriorated. I noticed that many of the buildings that lined this man-made water network were built at odd angles, or at least they now looked that way. Window frames were slanted and roofs didn't quite align correctly. Many of the tall, narrow buildings were painted in bright colours, adding to their eccentric appearance. I'd like to think that this also went someway to explaining my muffin-induced experiences of the previous summer.

It was gone nine when I got back to the hostel. My room still housed a collection of passed-out travellers, and the haze created by the crowd of smokers outside gave me little reason to hang around. I found a computer, booked up a couple of nights accommodation for my onward travels and then headed back out on to Nieuwendijk, this time turning left towards the station. The series of alleyways that branch off this main shopping street were now illuminated with green and red neon signs, and the crowds of people that had been walking along the canals earlier now appeared to be situated in the many bars and restaurants around this part of town. It was starting to spit with rain again, so I peeled off the street and stepped into a small establishment on the right hand side, reasoning with myself that I could have one quick drink before going to bed before my early start in the morning.

I was surprised at how empty it was as I ordered a beer and took a seat at the bar. There were a couple of people camped out on a small table at the far end of the narrow room, and one other man further along the bar nursing a dark ale, but otherwise it was empty. Some obscure European sports programming was being shown silently on a screen that hung on the wall in the corner, whilst quiet music played from a laptop being controlled by the bar lady. It all felt a bit dull and subdued, but then I wasn't going to stay long.

Two hours later and the situation had changed a little. I'd got chatting to the other man at the bar, Jimmy. He had been on his way back home to the U.S. after a family get together in his native Ireland, but his connecting flight had been delayed and so he had an unexpected free evening in Amsterdam, which he was spending getting to know the draught selection at this particular establishment. It turned out that he part-owned and ran an Irish pub and restaurant in Phoenix, Arizona. He had gone out there when he was younger having gotten fed up of life in Ireland, and then decided not to go back. He told me about how his was one of the first Irish pubs to open in Phoenix, although their popularity had caught on and there were now several competing with his. Jimmy was quite a bit older than me, and had lots of interesting stories to tell. His cheerful nature and approach to life was exactly what being out and travelling is all about. I sat there, happily sharing travel adventures with him as our pint glasses quickly emptied. He wasn't shy of keeping them topped up either, and soon I found myself leaning against the bar beyond casualness, and more out of necessity as I battled to remain upright on the high stool.

'Come over to the cabin!' he said at one point, deep into the evening.

This seemed like an odd invitation even in my slightly inebriated state, but before I had too much time to contemplate whether I was being invited on some bizarre rural retreat, Jimmy had stood up and was heading towards the gloomy area at the back of the bar. Out of curiosity I slid gracefully off my stool and stumbled after him, where to my surprise I found a self-contained wooden cabin. We stepped inside and Jimmy pulled out a self-rolled cigarette. He lit it and took a couple of puffs before handing it to me.

'Here, get some of that down you.'

As previously mentioned, I do not smoke, but there is something about the Irish that is very difficult to argue with, and so I took a quick drag, which did little to aid my balancing issues, and went some way to explaining why my route back to the bar was far less efficient than it should have been. Once I had made it back, and was once again precariously balanced on the stool, I found an Australian lady had joined us.

Kim was a 'life coach' who was on holiday exploring Europe. She again was a little older than myself, and took great pleasure in mocking my apparent youth. I in turn quizzed her extensively about what a 'life coach' was, to the point where she handed me her business card. On the back it read 'Branch out. Reach for the sky. Let yourself grow'. This was all too much for me to understand in my current state, so I semi fell off my stool and went to the toilet. It was here that I encountered a tap system the likes of which I had never experienced before, and honestly hope never to again. As I accurately explained to my new drinking buddies upon my return, I couldn't work out how to 'make water happen'. I eventually cracked the complex system, finally discovering that you had to press down the base of the tap to 'make water happen'. At least they now knew I was the hand-washing type, and a determined one at that. I also found on my return that the bar looked very different to when I had left. Granted the tap complications had meant my trip had taken a little longer than usual, but this felt like a different place. It turned out that a large thick green curtain had been pulled across the door and window at the front of the bar. I was now in a lock-in.

The drinks continued to flow between our tri-national group. Our different backgrounds and reasons for being temporarily united in a small bar in Amsterdam keeping us entertained until I decided that I should really be heading off. It was getting on for three in the morning, and I knew I had a very long day ahead of me tomorrow. I made my apologies, and after briefly getting tangled in the curtain, the bar lady unlocked the door and released me back on to the streets. I stumbled the short distance to my hostel and headed for my room, where I found the black hostel cat standing guard by the door. This was a little disturbing, but I did my best not to let it phase me whilst I battled with the electronic swipe card as I fought to gain entry into my room. I silently got myself sorted before climbing into my bunk, with the thick, smoky air helping to knock me out before my head had hit the pillow. My journey to Copenhagen was due to take 12 hours, and the evening's antics had probably not been the best preparation.

Chapter 7

Amsterdam to Duisburg

The morning arrived a little quicker than I would have liked. Thankfully the thick herbal smog meant I was probably quite stoned as I dragged myself from the bunk and fell down the small metal ladder, so I was largely unaware of the inconvenience of only having had three hours sleep. The shower went someway to restore my sobriety, and after descending the steps to the cave-like underground breakfast area (passing the black cat once again on the stairs) I was soon fed and ready to set off.

I headed south through the centre to the canals for a morning stroll. The sun had returned, vividly enhancing the vibrant colours of the abstract, slanting building fascias as I zig-zagged over bridges and along the waterways. I came across a small market square hidden behind a cluster of buildings. The enclosed courtyard was filled with tatty stalls selling fresh vegetables, with early morning shoppers milling around as they stocked up for the week. I then began heading back towards the station via Oudezijds Voorburgwal; a quintessentially picturesque canal-lined street. As I walked along it, admiring the bridges and quirky building fronts that overlooked them, my enjoyment of the quiet morning ambience was suddenly broken by the sound of an aggressive knock on a nearby window. I looked up to the right and saw a rather scantily clad lady pressed up against a pane of glass on the first floor, surrounded by red fluorescent bulbs and making gestures not befitting of such an early morning hour. I turned around and disappeared along a nearby alleyway, and after a few tricky moments of negotiating tram lines, busy roads and bike lanes I was back in Amsterdam Centraal station.

Despite it only being a fleeting visit to the Dutch capital, I was satisfied that I had glimpsed a broad selection of Amsterdam's contrasting cultural offerings and I was ready to continue on my Euro-train adventure. I checked the departure board and found the platform I needed. Then, a couple of minutes before 10, ICE train number 123 pulled up. There are helpful diagrams that tell you where along the platform you need to be stood to board the correct part of these long international services, and so I was perfectly placed to reach out and press the 'open door' button on carriage 21. There was an exciting hydraulic whoosh as a small metal step emerged from beneath the carriage and the large door slid open. This was a German train and so I had high expectations. I was not disappointed. I felt like train passenger royalty, even though I was wearing a creased t-shirt and heavily scuffed shoes. Inside the modern train I was greeted by a slick interior. Wooden panelling and neatly upholstered flooring led me along to my designated seat - seat 83 - where, of course, someone was already sitting. A middle-aged man stuttered a few lines in German before indicating that he wanted to sit with his friend and asked if I could sit in his seat a few rows back. I emitted my best weary German sigh and shuffled along the carriage. We pulled out of Amsterdam Centraal at exactly 10 o'clock. My long day on the trains had begun.

The train continued to impress as we zoomed through the Dutch countryside. The speed at which the trees shot by the window suggested that we were travelling at some speed, but from within the calm surrounds of the luxurious carriage there was no obvious indication that we were moving at all. The train felt like it was gliding above the rails, and as I let my head sink into the headrest pillow attachment I envisaged a far less arduous day on the tracks than I had originally anticipated. I then realised that I had some important admin to attend to. I dragged my head away from the cushioning and delved into my bag to pull out my newly valid InterRail pass. This was an exciting moment, and I eagerly pulled down the table from the seat back in front and opened up the glossy pages. The first job was to mark off the date of travel on the airline style ticket that was stapled in the front. I did this swiftly on the tiny space provided and then skimmed down to the section where I had to provide extra details about the journey. I filled out the departure point and destination, then the departure time and train number. Just as I was finishing off my neat ticket annotations a friendly-faced man in a uniform appeared beside me to check on my progress. I proudly held it out to him like a schoolboy who had finished his homework a day early, and he duly stamped it with his ticket validating machine and handed it back to me with a smile. I was now a fully-fledged *InterRailer*! I relaxed back into my seat, slipping in my earphones just as the man who had displaced me from my original seat reservation was beginning a rather defensive speech with the ticket inspector a few rows in front. Serves him bloody right.

The time and miles flew by, with the only slightly uncomfortable moment coming during a brief stop at Arnhem, where a man on the platform suddenly pressed his face up against the window next to me. He looked a little sadistic and having his smudged facial features so close to mine was quite alarming, so I was grateful when we pulled away without him onboard. Around two hours after leaving Amsterdam the train pulled up in Duisburg, western Germany. This was my first change of the day, and after reluctantly decamping from the comfortable surrounds of the ICE train I headed down into the large underground walkway beneath the platforms. It was lunchtime, and as I was in Germany I thought it was a good time to deploy one of my finest German lines. I found a small kiosk and stepped up to the window.

'Ein bratwurst mit brot, bitte!'

A large freshly griddled sausage and a bread roll were then quickly delivered into my hand in exchange for a couple of Euros. I had about an hour before my next connection, so I took my lunch outside and ate up the classic German cuisine whilst I strolled around the expansive concrete forecourt in front of the station. A few 60s-looking office blocks were dotted about, with several slightly dilapidated billboards hanging above the adjacent roads. It didn't look like the most inspiring destination, and so after finishing my lunch I decided to use the remaining time before my next train in a practical manner, and so I headed inside to the ticket office. I was running to quite a tight schedule, and so I thought I would try and book up my next couple of journeys. I joined the short queue, standing behind a man with a massive suitcase that had 'Travelite' on the badge. After a few minutes of queuing I was called up to the counter and quickly began confusing the man behind it as I mixed German words in with English. After a few minutes of frowns and computer keyboard tapping I was handed some tickets and seat reservations. Aside from my linguistic deviances it was a very efficient process, and soon I had seat reservations for the next few onward journeys, which was a relief (even if my seats always seemed to be occupied). I came out of the ticket office very satisfied with my efficient use of time as I awaited my next train. In fact I was so pleased with what I had achieved in my brief stop in Germany that I decided to purchase some celebratory sweets. I stepped into a little confectionary shop and found the ideal offering: a small blue packet that had 'Professional Mints' written in large letters on the front. This was very fitting, as I had been very professional in my efficient travel arrangements. I was about to head over to the cashier's desk when I suddenly noticed that my flies were undone. In my excitement at arranging more international train journeys I had obviously forgotten to zip them up after a quick trip to the toilet. This somewhat ruined my professionalism, so I put the fancy pack of mints back on the shelf and bought some Tic Tacs instead.

Back out in the expansive underground walkway I approached a screen that displayed the upcoming departures. I scanned the list of destinations, casually flicking a Tic Tac around my mouth with my tongue as I did so. I smiled as I found the destination I was looking for. The 13.46 to Hamburg would leave from platform 13. Ha! I thought to myself; platform 13 – unlucky for some! Not me though, because my journey was going *excellently*, and this after all was the German rail network – the finest and most efficient railway service in the world! A word flashed up next to the Hamburg service; 'Verspätung' it read. This was nice – a little German phrase that probably meant 'have a lovely journey on our excellent railway service!' to see you off before you board one of their fantastic and reliable trains. I headed up to platform 13 and dropped my bag down. There were quite a few people around, many with suitcases and also slightly confused expressions on their faces. I sighed knowingly. I understood that not everyone would be as efficient and in control of their journey planning as I had demonstrated here, but in time they would learn and become wise like me.

After a few minutes stood slowly wearing down the mint in my mouth, I noticed that people were gathering beneath the departure board that hung from the platform roof. The puzzled faces were out in force, and they were now being accompanied my some head scratching. I wandered over to see what was causing the confusion. The train listing was still there, with the kindly message still flashing away next to the word 'Hamburg'. Although it was now flashing red. At the bottom of the screen there was now also a scrolling message that included the words 'dreißig minuten'. Now I joined in the puzzledness. Why 30 minutes? *What* was 30 minutes? I was pretty sure the journey was several hours. Maybe they had decided to enhance the service having learnt about the long journey I was undertaking and had kindly decided to speed up this leg to make it easier on me. A slightly flustered looking station employee hurried out of a nearby booth and was immediately descended upon by a rabble of luggage-wielding passengers. Some angry words appeared to be exchanged, with one standing out in particular. It was in English, and its use made me stop chewing on my mint. The word was 'delay'. It didn't take long for me to then make the horrible realisation. 'Verspätung' meant *delay*. I took a sharp intake of breath as its significance dawned on me. Unfortunately this sucked the Tic Tac into my windpipe causing me to mildly choke, with the resulting cough in turn sending the mint firing out of my mouth and bouncing off along the platform. This was bad news. *Very* bad news. The delay that is, not the loss of the mint, because I had plenty more of those in my pocket.

A 30 minute delay in itself was not a big deal. I'd certainly faced longer in my travels, but it was the onward implications that were now a major concern. This train journey was the second of three that I was booked on today to get to Copenhagen, and it was also the journey that had the tightest turnaround at the other end. There was a 20 minute window between this train arriving in Hamburg and the next train leaving for Copenhagen. I did a swift calculation in my head and worked out that even if the arrival and departure platforms in Hamburg were adjacent, minus 10 minutes would not be enough time to make the train. I walked back over to the pillar I had been standing by and considered what this meant. I'd been offered three possible departure times the previous day, but I had chosen the latest one to allow me the most time in Amsterdam as my visit had already been cut short by not being able to take the night train. I presumed this meant that missing the final connection from Hamburg would leave me unable to make it to Denmark today. This would not only mess up my hostel booking and leave me homeless in Hamburg, but it would also ruin the onward trains I had so efficiently booked just minutes before. From everything seeming to come together so neatly, it was now all going horribly wrong. Thanks platform 13.

As I dispensed another mint into my hand, hoping that its refreshing vapours would help clear the situation, a man in ridiculously tight lilac trousers came up to me and muttered something about Hamburg. I nodded, which seemed to satisfy him, and he sauntered off again to the other side of the platform. I went over to the now less hassled train attendant and enquired about the train's status. He also started muttering dismissively, said the word 'Hamburg' quite loudly, and then waved me away. Finally a woman came up to me, apparently intrigued by my Englishness, and began telling me how her daughter had been to Windsor and that it was nice. She also said that Hamburg was nice. I in turn told her that it was very windy - which it wasn't - but other than telling her that I had blue eyes, a small chicken and that I liked eating ballpoint pens, my knowledge of German left me with little else to pursue the conversation with.

The result of these fleeting encounters left me with the distinct impression that I would be spending significantly more time in Hamburg than I'd intended. This was quite the predicament as I had nowhere to stay in the city, and I had to be in other cities – other countries even – during the following few days. My plans had fallen apart in one simple word; 'Verspätung'. It was now easily my least favourite word in the German dictionary. It was then compounded as the Verspätung grew to 'fünfundvierzig minuten'. This was all very unwelcome, and while we're on the subject, very un-German.

The train creaked slowly into the station 50 minutes later, almost as if it was trying to slip in unnoticed, knowing that it had shamed itself with this uncharacteristic delay. It had more reason to be ashamed too, because this was no ICE train, this was a very crappy looking train. The only solace I had taken in this journey-wrecking delay was that at least I would be transported to my now final destination of the day in style and comfort, but it wasn't to be. For a start the carriages were numbered in an inexplicable manner: 9, 8, 5 and 4. This was surely madness at its most prevalent. After positioning myself so carefully at the correct part of the platform over the long course of the delay, I then found myself desperately rushing up and down beside the train as I tried to work out this bizarre labelling system. I eventually hauled myself up the rusty steps and into a grimy, battered carriage, one along from where it turned out I needed to be. I then once again found my seat occupied, this time by an angry elderly gentleman in a suit as battered as our surrounds. I paused beside the seat and the man turned and glared at me, before fiercely shouting a few words in his native tongue. I was quite taken aback, but quickly a lady from further along the carriage hurried over and led me away to a free seat on the other side. I slumped against the murky, scratched window, thoroughly fed up as we bumped uncomfortably and noisily out of the station. My preconceptions about German rail travel had been thoroughly tarnished.

Chapter 8

Duisburg to Copenhagen

A few hours later and my mood had brightened a little, but this may have been due to the number of times I'd hit my head against the window, which could have dislodged any memories of the problems I now faced. I'd resigned myself to spending the night in Hamburg, and only hoped that it wasn't so much of a summer hotspot that I wouldn't be able to find accommodation for the night. As we pulled into Hamburg an announcement came spluttering over the tannoy. It was difficult to decipher, partly because it was in German, but also because the poor sound quality suggested the speaker covers hid little more than two cups linked by a piece of string as a communication system. I thought however, that I caught the words 'Kobenhavn' and 'sieben' being mentioned amongst the rapid-fire gurgling. It was one minute past six. A glimmer of hope had surfaced.

I hurried off the train, glad to be free of its dated interior and miserable clientele. If the announcement had indeed made reference to a train to Copenhagen at around seven then I didn't have long to find it and sort out my ticket, and the task would be even trickier thanks to the sprawling mass that formed Hamburg central railway station. It was hugely busy as it was rush hour, and people were whizzing past in every direction, seemingly as keen as me to be somewhere else very urgently. I clambered up a set of stairs and found myself on a mezzanine level, none the wiser as to where the ticket office was. I ducked through the crowds and along little passageways between food outlets and tour kiosks, well aware that my imminent travel plans were hanging in the balance. Eventually I spotted an encouraging sign that I followed around a few more corners until I caught sight of a glass-fronted reception area with a familiar looking digital number display prominently fixed against the back wall. I dived through the automatic doors and snatched a ticket from the dispenser. I checked my ticket and then the screen. There was a difference of 28 between the two between. I took a seat, drumming my fingers on the plastic padding of the seat cushioning and tapping my feet in agitation. There were lots of other people waiting for tickets and information, but I sensed none were suspended in a strange international no-man's land as I currently felt that I was. An agonising 15 minutes later and my number finally flashed up on the screen. I hurried up to the desk and quickly explained my situation.

'Okay, ja das ist no problem. Zair ist one more train to København tonight at seven twenty-eight. I can exchange your ticket for free.'

There was that decisive German efficiency that had been lacking earlier.

And so it was done, and there was much rejoicing.

I was back on track, or at least I would be in 45 minutes. Suddenly after all the anxiousness and frantic running about I now had a bit of time to kill. I wandered back along the upper mezzanine level and found a balcony that looked out over the platforms beneath the giant arched roof of the station. It was undoubtedly an impressive structure. Sure, it didn't have the class or finesse of the newly restored St Pancras, but the dark, imposing metal trusses still gave a sense of foreboding grandeur that was intriguing to the eye. As I stood surveying the busy scenes below I suddenly felt a tap on my shoulder. I turned around to find two girls standing there, one tightly clutching a bunch of flowers.

'Are you Oliver?' the girl with the flowers tentatively enquired.

I wasn't, and I politely told them this.

'Oh,' she said, looking a little disappointed, 'we are supposed to meet him for our friend'.

I again apologetically confirmed that I was still not the person that they were looking for, and wished them luck as they scurried off in search of other lone males who could be the elusive Oliver.

From my fantastic vantage point I soon noticed that a crowd was beginning to build on platform 8, and so I left the mezzanine level and headed back down the steps to join it. A train soon arrived and people dragged themselves up off their bags ready to board. Then, just before half past seven, the train left. At no point had the doors opened and there had not been any announcements. Not for the first time today, expressions of bewilderment broke out across the faces of those gathered along the platform. København then disappeared from the platform's departure board. Things had taken another negative turn on this day of rail-related ups and downs. I overheard some mutterings from nearby would-be passengers about 'gleise sieben'. I moved across to platform 7, where I got chatting to Matthias, who was off to visit friends in the Danish capital. As a German national he seemed like a good ally to have in these times of confusion.

It was now comfortably past half seven and concern was growing. Why there hadn't been any announcements was a mystery, and no one was too sure where to go. Eventually a station employee nonchalantly wandered down on to the platform, apparently oblivious to any sort of time-tabling problem. I walked over, as did others, and between the group of us the simple question was posed: 'København?'

'Gleise funf' the man replied, shaking his head as if we were all idiots for not realising that they had moved the train's arrival point and time without advertising it anywhere.

Another frantic few moments followed as word spread amongst the crowd about the new departure platform. Everyone then quickly collected up their luggage and hurried up the steps, scurrying over the bridge and then dropping back down to platform 5 on the other side. Sure enough there was a train there, albeit a very short one, with just four carriages. So far the international services I had been on had been very long affairs, and I couldn't understand why this one wasn't, especially given the number of people on the platform. A guard from the train was encouraging haste from the deluge of new arrivals, clearly keen to get the train moving. This hardly seemed fair given the lack of information and numerous platform changes, but everyone did their best to pile their stuff onboard as quickly as possible. At 7.41 the train edged out of the station, a sense of calm and relief having returned after a hectic few minutes. It was a Danish train, Matthias informed me, and once we were inside the padded interior dampened any of the audible fuss that had proceeded boarding. I was in the end carriage, which was surprisingly empty given the crowds that had surged on to the platform moments earlier. I took my aisle seat, dropping my collection of tickets on to the wooden table that stretched out from below the window as I settled in for the final leg of the day's turbulent journey.

The scenery changed as the evening slipped quietly towards night. The sunset brought a deep orange sky that sat over the fields of northern Germany as we powered along. An elderly Danish lady took her place in the seat next to mine, and soon began telling me in broken English about her reason for being on the train. From what I could establish she was born in Namibia, but worked for a bank in

Stuttgart for many years. She had just been back there to visit her daughter, and it was with some sadness that she couldn't make it down there more often. She also told me that she hoped to make a visit to Namibia next year, although it would be tough because of her age. It was nice talking to her, although I felt sorry for her, as she was clearly disappointed to be heading home, far away from her family.

Soon water appeared outside of the window, and then on the other side too; we were heading out to the islands! As the light faded we pulled up at a rural station. The lady next to me got off, and as I helped her with her bags she asked if I was going on the ferry. I smiled and told her that I was, but only out of politeness, because I had no intention of going on a ferry tonight.

With the darkness meaning there was little to see out of the window, I had pulled out my book when an announcement came over the train's speakers. It was delivered in Danish, German and English, although I was paying little attention. It was the last few words that caught my ear, however, as some instruction seemed to be given that indicated we must leave the train, but that we could leave our belongings on board. I looked up and saw a large, grubby white wall next to the train on one side. We had slowed to a crawling pace as the other passengers in the carriage began rallying together their belongings and heading towards the door. I didn't understand what was happening; there was no way we were at Copenhagen already. We ground to a stop and a short queue built up at the carriage door. With seemingly little option I grabbed my jacket along with a couple of things from my bag and stood up. I followed the slow moving line to the doorway and stepped down out of the carriage. I looked around, squinting slightly at the brightly lit, stark surrounds that were in contrast to the soft, dimly lit carriage interior. There was only a narrow gap to squeeze along as the train had stopped next to a row of cars, with more rows of cars forming as I followed the other passengers, weaving around the vehicles towards the far wall. We were in what looked remarkably like the vehicle loading area of a ship. This was very peculiar. I stepped through a metal door and into a stairwell, where I climbed up a few levels before coming out into a large seating area. My suspicions grew as I noticed a 'deck plan' map on the wall beside me. I walked along past a shop and a restaurant and then found a large glass door. As a final piece of confirmation I opened the heavy door and was immediately blasted by a strong gust of salty sea breeze. I fought my way across the dark space in font of me and found myself up against a railing. In front of me was an expanse of water, with a few reddish streaks of fading sunlit sky in the distance. I was now convinced that we were on a ferry. A loud blast of the horn and we started moving off into the darkness.

Despite the bracing wind that was sweeping up off the waters, it was a warm summer evening, and I spent this novel and unexpected (but very welcome) addition to my day on the trains strolling around the decks to stretch my legs. I knew Copenhagen was situated on an island to the east of mainland Denmark, but I assumed that we reached this via a series of tunnels and bridges. This development also explained the short train length, because it had to fit on the boat.

Forty-five minutes later and we were instructed to return to our vehicles. I bumped into Matthias on the way down to the train, and he said I should come along to the front carriage where there was a group gathering to have a few drinks. I stopped off back at my seat to drop off a few things and then edged my way through the train as it set off back on to more familiar tracks. In the front carriage I found lively discussions going on between a group that included a German, a Dane, a Norwegian and two Swedes. I took a seat and was quickly handed a beer from an open crate on the table. Soon we were chatting away, happily discussing the various merits and complications of the selection of languages that were on offer between the group. Daniel, the softly spoken Dane who was sat next to me then unexpectedly announced that he was returning from a five-day martial arts seminar in Harborg that was hosted by 'The Master', who had travelled over on a rare visit from China. He then went on to talk about the Danish faction of Hell's Angels. Appearances can certainly be deceptive.

From seemingly out of nowhere (but probably his bag) the Norwegian man pulled out a large spirit bottle, and even more impressively, a stack of plastic shot glasses. These Scandinavians come prepared. The shot glasses got duly filled and handed out. I have no idea what it was, but it was strong and no doubt highly flammable. I pulled out a pack of cards, and between these, the drink and the lively conversations, the time flew by. A train employee then came swaying along the aisle, but far from wanting to stop our antics, he just wanted to check our tickets. I realised I had left mine in my bag back in the rear carriage, and so I headed back to find them, briefly impeded by an uncooperative automatic door that refused to let me through, much to the amusement of a Chinese couple sitting beside it. Once I had got back to my seat, located my filled-out pass and shown it to the guard, the train was pulling up at Copenhagen station. It was 12.18 in the morning, a little over 14 hours since I'd set off from Amsterdam.

Outside I strapped on my bag and pulled out a scrap of paper from my pocket. I'd booked the hostel back in Amsterdam and had drawn a quick sketch of the roads I needed to navigate along in order to reach my accommodation for the night. I stopped under a streetlight outside of the station to check where I needed to go. I set off down Tietgensgade and walked beside a fence where through occasional gaps I could see the eerie, silhouetted form of a themepark. The streets were near deserted except for the occasional cyclist whirring along in the darkness. I crossed a bridge over a canal and turned off along a side street. A bit of zig-zagging and I was soon crossing Strøget, which was a much busier street with a few bars along it that were dispensing some rowdy late night revellers into the surround roads. I crossed over, passing a man urinating against a stone pillar, but unlike in Brussels, no one seemed to deem this sight worthy of a photograph.

In a neighbouring road I found my hostel; a smart, modern looking building with a brightly illuminated sign. Inside I got checked in and headed up to my room. I was shattered and looking forward to getting my head down for a few hours after a fraught day crossing three countries (and a bit of sea). Unfortunately I was arriving at a less than sociable hour, and I now faced a battle to locate my bed in a large, dark dorm room. I swiped the keycard against the door and slowly edged it open. A crack of bright light was sent cutting through the pitch-black room from the corridor, revealing a glimpse of what was inside. Clothes littered the floor between tightly packed bunk beds, the mounds of sheets covering the unmistakable forms of sleeping backpackers. I quickly closed the door behind me and tip-toed through the room. Being summer it was busy, so the odds were that there was only going to be one spare bed: bed eight – the one indicated on my hostel receipt. I peered around as my eyes adjusted to the minimal light, eventually finding my way to the far end of the room. It looked like a 12 bed dorm, and to my great relief I found what I sincerely hoped was an empty bottom bunk. I silently got ready for bed, cleaning my teeth in a nearby sink and making up the sheets as part of an intricate operation of silence. Once done, I climbed into the bed, smacking my head on an inconveniently placed glass screen at the top end of the bunk as I did so. Slightly dazed, I looked up as a bit of light crept in underneath the loosely flapping curtain and caught on the sheet of glass. There was a large number '8' printed on it. Well at least I was in the right place. I let my head fall heavily on to the pillow, and quite possibly helped by the mild concussion, I was asleep in seconds.

Chapter 9

Copenhagen, Denmark

The next morning I tucked into a much appreciated buffet breakfast. The building far more resembled an office block than a hostel, and the piles of rubble and machinery in the glass-fronted courtyard suggested it hadn't long been in existence. I retuned to my room after filling my stomach to pack up my small amount of belongings. I then dropped my bag in a bathroom next to reception that was oddly doubling up as a luggage store, and set off into the city.

I walked up through Copenhagen's main square, Kongens Nytorv (King's New Square) with its cobbled pedestrianised areas and statue of Christian V – the former King of Denmark and Norway - sitting on a horse. I wandered around the square before turning into Nyhavn, which is arguably one of the prettiest streets in Europe, and the former home of the ever popular Danish poet and writer, Hans Christian Andersen. Two rows of colourfully painted cafes and restaurants line the canal that runs in a straight line along to the harbour from Kongens Nytorv, and being the height of summer, the eateries were spilling out across the cobbles with tables and chairs filling the space beneath expansive canopies. Despite it still only being mid-morning they were already filling up fast with tourists sampling the fresh seafood and wide selection of beverages on offer. Those that weren't yet on the hunt for refreshments were shuffling about trying to capture the setting in the best light on their cameras, while others lined up along the narrow promenades in preparation for a boat trip on one of the little charter vessels that were vying for space in the limited mooring area. I weaved my way through the crowds to a bridge that crossed over the waterway further along Nyhavn, briefly taking in the picturesque setting as the sun behind me lit up the vibrant red, yellow, green and blue painted buildings. I moved on, turning north along the waterway at the end of Nyhavn. It was time to focus on my main Danish mission - the specific reason why I had come to Copenhagen. I had some important unfinished business in the city that I needed to put right.

It had been a fun few days in Toronto. I was making use of some free flight vouchers I'd acquired having given up my seat on a flight home on a previous visit. It was mid December and I'd just landed myself a new job, and so I was taking a break having saved up some leave before finishing my contract. I had no real plans for my budget trip to Canada, but ended up meeting some friendly people whose company was far more warming than the temperature outside. Snow and ice lined the city streets, and at minus 11 degrees centigrade, plus a bone tingling minus 17 degree wind-chill, it was probably the coldest place I had been to. Thankfully I'd remembered my hat, so the weather didn't prove too much of a problem. That was until I came to fly home.

I arrived at Lester B. Pearson International Airport with plenty of time to spare before my flight. Unfortunately I was greeted by a very long and agitated queue, and I soon discovered that whilst Toronto was coping with its cold weather, London wasn't. The temperature had dropped to around freezing in the UK, and a few snowflakes had meandered down from the sky and come to rest on Heathrow's runways. This had caused chaos, and as a result some flights had been cancelled – mine included. Eventually, a not-especially-friendly airline employee told us that we would be lucky to make it home for New Year, let alone Christmas, which was five days away. I wasn't overly concerned about the prospect of being away for Christmas (in fact it sounded quite exciting), but as I was only there on free flights as a cheap getaway, I couldn't afford to stay on indefinitely, and the airline wasn't about to subsidise my unexpected holiday extension. I sat in the terminal building for a couple of hours whilst others rushed around waving hundreds of dollars in the air as they tried to secure a seat on any other flight to London they could find. I eventually called the free phone number for the airline after the madness had died down and enquired about alternative flights. I was told that there was a flight two days later to Copenhagen, and that I could have my ticket switched for free. This sounded like an exciting alternative. I eagerly accepted the offer, and the switch was made there and then over the phone. I then took the train back to the hostel to have a couple more enjoyable days wandering around Toronto with the people I'd met there, before setting off for Denmark.

On the flight I got chatting to a Danish family, and not knowing anything about the city I asked what I should do there. They said to visit the Little Mermaid. I thought this was a film, or at best a fictitious creature, and so I didn't hold up much hope of achieving this, but I thanked them anyway. The family then invited me to stay with them in their home for Christmas if I couldn't get back to London, which was incredibly kind of them. I immediately liked the Danish, and so I promised I would do my best at finding this mermaid creature during what I intended to be a fleeting visit.

It was a mere minus six degrees in Copenhagen, although the roads and pavements were far less adapted for the conditions than Toronto's had been. After a comfortable night's sleep in a centrally located hostel I managed to slip and slide my way along the icy streets and out beyond the harbour to where this mermaid was apparently to be found. Understandably it was pretty empty on the roads as the Danes prepared for their festive celebrations. The exposed promenades by the waters edge were under attack from a severely bitter wind, and as I battled with the tough conditions I lost some sense of direction, but I eventually caught sight of what I understood to be a statue of the Little Mermaid. It was a little disappointing, and also confusing as it seemed to look nothing like how I imagined a mermaid would look, not least because it was being transported on what in the heavy snow appeared to be a chariot being pulled by an angry-faced bull. I was never that up to scratch on my fairy tales though, and it was very cold and my hands were going numb, so I didn't want to hang around worrying about minor details. I just about managed to withdraw my icy fingers from my gloves and take a quick picture as evidence of my achievements, before sliding my way back to the warmer surrounds of the airport where I found a flight that would take me back to London. I very conveniently arrived back home at half past 11 at night on Christmas Eve, much to the surprise of my family, who I hadn't kept fully in the loop about my impromptu Danish interlude. All in all I thought it had been a very successful festive excursion, having defeated the odds in making it back for Christmas *and* having seen the apparently famous Little Mermaid.

A couple of days later I was regaling my tale of adventure to friends, but as I showed the photo of the mermaid I was interrupted by one of them after she had given me a dubious frown.

'That isn't the Little Mermaid,' she said flatly, which I found a little insulting given the battle I'd had to find it.

'Yes it is!' I protested, 'it just looks a bit odd because it has a lot of snow on it.'

It was a strong argument, I'm sure you would agree.

'No – the Little Mermaid has a tail!'

'It's hidden by the snow!'

'And it isn't pulled on a chariot by an angry-faced bull!'

Copenhagen, Denmark

'It's a post-modern interpretation!'

'And it sits on a rock in the water!' she persisted.

Oh.

I was then quickly presented with an internet image of the *actual* Little Mermaid statue: sitting on a rock in the water, with a tail, and looking decidedly un-angry. In fact it looked very mermaid-like. It was now painfully clear that I had been to the wrong statue. To rub salt into the wound I then discovered that I'd missed out on the real Little Mermaid statue by about a hundred metres. This irritated me greatly.

So here I was, back in Copenhagen a little under two years later, and in *much* more favourable weather. I wouldn't make the same mistake twice. I cut through what appeared to be a temporary entertainment venue set up by the waterside for summer festivities, and then walked along Larsens Plads, where I passed an impressive looking yacht that two men were dangling off on ropes as they cleaned its shiny white exterior. Sparkling gold lettering gave the name as 'Starfire', which is a pretty cool name for a boat, if not especially nautical. In the distance, much further along the water I caught sight of an even bigger ship – a cruise liner. I paused. Where there are cruise liners, there are usually hoards of tourists. Not just normal tourists either, but *cruise* tourists; often elder couples (not wanting to adhere to stereotypes too much, or anything) and probably in a reduced state of normal functionality, having no doubt spent several days at sea being blindly told what to do whilst everything is handed to them (often quite literally) on a plate. As my thoughts drifted towards the impending threat of mass-tourist invasion, I suddenly became aware of a familiar looking statue to my left. It was the bull and chariot ensemble, proudly staged high up on a plinth with people passing it by without giving it a second glance. I scowled and carried on walking. I had to concede that it really had been a bit of a stupid error on my part to confuse this statue with a mermaid, even with the mentally and physically demanding weather conditions that I'd had to content with. And then I saw what I had been dreading. I walked around a bend in the pathway and there up ahead was a terrifying mass of colour. The cruise-shippers had clearly made it to shore, and they were now gathered around what I had to assume was the Little Mermaid statue. I suppose the benefit of this was that I now knew exactly where it was, but the down side was that I still might not get to see it as it was hidden in the crowd of bumbag wearing, camera swinging cruise-enthusiasts.

As I got closer I managed to glimpse the statue that had eluded me before. I'm not surprised I missed it, it's tiny! But then I suppose that is alluded to in its name.

The four-foot statue was commissioned in 1909, in tribute to the fish-lady character from the ballet by Hans Christian Andersen, *The Little Mermaid*. Apparently (as with Belgium's famous little statue) it has suffered at the hands of vandals and has had numerous limbs pinched over the years, including several decapitations, which isn't very 'fairytale' at all, really. It has also been blown off its perch with explosives, covered in paint and dressed in clothes in a series of odd political protests. All in all it has had a pretty tough life, although it did get a holiday to China a couple of years ago when it was temporarily moved over there for 'Expo 2010' in Shanghai.

Sat on a rock just off the shoreline on this bright summer's morning it was being mobbed by people determined to picture it from every conceivable angle. The more adventurous ones were even jumping across the rocks to the plinth where the mermaid sat to put their hand around it for a photo, selfishly ruining everyone else's shots. I grudgingly dropped down the slope and entered the

84

throngs of chattery people, clearly excited about being on day release from the ship. Balanced precariously on a rock I peered at the screen on my camera as I manoeuvred the lens in between the bodies to try and capture a clear shot. Just as I thought I had it perfectly lined up, the viewfinder was filled with a bright green presence.

'You take my picture?!'

An excitable man in ridiculous sunglasses and the obligatory bumbag stood before me, a stupid green polo shirt failing to cover the lower regions of his sizeable stomach – a stomach that was no doubt baffled by this sudden and strenuous rock-stepping activity that had been so unfairly thrust upon it after days of all-you-can-eat buffet meals and lying around on deck. I snatched the camera and took the photo, and after watching another man awkwardly leap over to the rock and balance precariously against the poor statue I began to wonder if I was fighting a lost cause. As I considered giving up on the all-important 'evidence shot', there was a loud, sharp cry from up on the promenade. A small woman in a straw hat was waving a little novelty flag on a stick high above her head and summoning the group. They were on the move! The effect of this shrill summons was brilliant. The tourists started muttering as they collected up their camera bags and relatives and began shuffling back up on to the walkway to join their leader. It was like a human version of Noah's Ark as they were herded up in their pairs to head back to the ship, leaving me alone to take the all-important photo, free of distraction and visual disturbance.

Click. Job done. My Danish mission was complete.

I scrambled back up the slope and headed over to the neighbouring Kastellet, a military post consisting of a collection of red-roofed buildings that sit hidden behind a large star-shaped grass bank with a moat running around the front of it. I stepped across the bridge and into the complex where I noticed a sign that amused me; 'no unplanned meetings' it read. I climbed up on to the grassy ramparts and made my way around the pentagonal pathway, admiring a nice little windmill that unexpectedly sits within its confines. I jogged most of the way as I knew I was going to be sat down on another long train journey soon, but also to prevent anyone talking to me, as I didn't want to be accused of meeting anyone as this would definitely have been unplanned, and therefore apparently in breech of Danish law.

With the Kastellet successfully circum-navigated, I climbed down from the bank and headed back over the bridge and off along Grønningen. I turned left at a busy junction and an area of parkland appeared to my right. I glimpsed a railway line through the bushes, before a pathway entrance emerged from the shrubbery. The railway line seemed to have vanished underground, and as I wound around some trees I caught sight of a large building that had big stone pillars at its front. It look like it was probably significant in some way, and this proved correct as I neared the grand entrance and read the sign on the front: this was the Statens Museum for Kunst - Denmark's largest art museum. After an efficient morning of mermaid hunting I was open for some further touristic distractions, and so I climbed the steps and went through into the large entrance foyer.

Other than some special exhibitions the museum appeared to be free to wander about in, and at the top of a staircase I found a number of large doorways that gave access to specific collections. I wandered through the halls observing various paintings, gazing wisely at impressionist pieces and intently reading the neatly translated descriptions to the side of striking portraits. The museum apparently contains nearly nine thousand paintings and sculptures, although to be honest I didn't count them. There were works by internationally renowned artists such as Picasso, Matisse and Rembrandt, but also a large representation from local painters. A personal favourite was a small oil on canvass dating from the 17th Century by Dutch artist, Adriaen Pietersz van de Venne. The painting, 'Hvor vi passer sammen', translates as 'How well we go together'. Based on the intriguing scene that had been skilfully depicted, I personally would have named it 'Two angry owls dressed in rags go ice skating'. It is probably with some relief for the arts world that I am not more heavily involved in it.

I moved on to a different gallery and found myself surrounded by very odd objects, such as a square marked out with masking tape on the floor with newspaper bundles attached to parachutes dumped within its borders. I guessed that I had entered the 'modern art' section of the museum. As part of another baffling exhibit I found myself cautiously pushing through some swing doors that I wasn't altogether convinced I should be going through, where inside I found a mock hospital ward, complete with two injured bodies lying in beds and hooked up to heart rate machines. This was weird. I don't really get modern art.

After half an hour of further contemporary-based confusion I came across a room that caught my interest, because it was an activity room! Now I am of course a grown up, but the chance to get stuck into something a bit more involved than just looking at things and confusing myself was an inviting prospect. I stepped inside and found the smallish room to be empty of people, but on the far side was a series of draws and wooden pots. Inside the draws I found sheets of A3 paper and wooden boards for leaning on. I took a board and a piece of paper, and then selected a pencil from one of the pots. This was obviously a classy establishment as they didn't just have the dregs of broken and chewed pencils that you may expect from a communal activity room, but instead it offered a full range of professional-looking lead-graphite 'art' pencils spanning the full H and B shade ranges. I chose a 'HB', which when I was younger I always thought was a brand of pencil, but now in my wise old age I know it to be an average, 'in-the-middle' sort of shade. I suspected 'average' would probably be the best outcome I could hope to achieve from any art I would create with it. Not that this was my first foray into the arts world...

I liked drawing from an early age. I used to like drawing cars, because I also really liked cars, but I also drew boats and planes, which I very much liked too. I suppose I was destined to travel, really. One afternoon when I was five years old I saw a competition in my local library. The challenge was to colour in a picture. Whilst I considered colouring in to be child's play compared to my favoured drawing, I was still keen to get involved and demonstrate my excellent pencil control. The picture itself was slightly peculiar, especially from a transport enthusiast's perspective, because entrants were required to colour in a picture of a frog in a bath. Now I had no specific skills in the frog or bath colouring-in fields, and I was also slightly perplexed, as even at five years old I knew baths were generally white and so this would require no colouring-in at all! Nevertheless I entered, and oddly enough I won the competition. It was a proud moment (as I'm sure my family would confirm) and having collected my prize of a small denomination of *Early Learning Centre* vouchers, I immediately headed to the shop to purchase what I had wanted for a long time: a beige model Land Rover. Yes, this is what I had my heart set on. Please don't let the drabness of this particular colour option influence your view of my personality, but this is what a neatly coloured-in frog in a bath had now facilitated. And what did I want the car for? I wanted to put it on my model toy farm of course!

Copenhagen, Denmark

Now you may be thinking that I have just subtly revealed to you my second passion of farming, but you would be wrong. Although I loved my model farm, I had absolutely no interest in farming. I spent my early years in suburban West London, which is certainly not an area synonymous with farming communities. As it happened I had no interest in the traditional aspects of a farm at all, but in fact what I really liked about it was the large barn and paddock area that allowed me to store vehicles, because as previously mentioned, vehicles were my area of interest. Forget the goats, the cows and the chickens - I had a tractor and a milk tanker, so *obviously* I needed a Land Rover to accompany them on my farm, and I got it, and all thanks to my first public venture into the art world.

So here I was, 20 years on and once again using my art skills for competitive endeavours. The sign said that the best pictures would be displayed on the 'drawings of the month' section of the website, which was very exciting. It also said the theme of the drawing should be 'man and beast'. This gave little scope for me to draw a car or a frog (or even a bath for that matter), so I sat down in a chair in the corner and contemplated what I could do instead. After a couple of minutes of intense artistic thought, I very cleverly decided that I would incorporate these two specific elements in a deeply metaphorical and symbolic manner, because I of course spend much of my time being deep and metaphorical. I began scribbling, keen to demonstrate that my art had progressed in the period since my frog and bath days. Soon other visitors started quietly entering the room, and upon seeing me hard at work they too began pulling out sheets of paper and settling down to draw. One of these people was a French lady (judging by her soft but heavily accented mutterings) who sat down armed with her chosen drawing equipment near the doorway. In a slightly disconcerting manner I noticed that she kept looking up at me in between focused glares at her paper. I wasn't sure which of 'man' or 'beast' I was offering inspiration for, but either way it was very off-putting, and so I quickly finished off my picture. I had skilfully combined both man and beast as required, sketching a picture of a train (as this was after all my reason for being out and about in Europe), but personifying it with a menacing glare. I softened this 'beast' element by giving it a mermaid's tail to represent 'beauty', whilst also keeping it topical with my current destination. I then in true artistic style named it something suitably off-kilter: 'Training the Beast on the Tracks of Beauty', which is so deep and metaphorical I don't fully understand it myself. As I walked across the room to drop off my no doubt soon-to-be-award-winning piece of artwork, I caught sight of the French lady's picture over her shoulder. I very much hoped that her repeated glances at me bore no reflection of her subject matter, as from what I could tell she was drawing a picture of a horse. I frowned, and then swiftly left the room.

It was now mid-afternoon, and time for me to move on from the Danish capital and catch the next train. I headed up through the busy main shopping street of Strøget, where I found a narrow gap in between the many ice-cream sellers and street entertainers to briefly peer inside the *Lego* shop as part of another heavily nostalgic nod towards my childhood, before moving on through the Town Hall Square and back to the station.

Unlike my experiences in Germany, the correct train pulled up at the correctly listed platform at the correctly scheduled time. It was another comfortable affair, with deeply padded grey seats and wooden armrests. As we pulled out of the station some dark clouds moved in overhead, a light smattering of rain soon lacing the window as we headed out onto the bridge that crosses the short stretch of sea between Copenhagen and Malmö, over the border in Sweden. Across the water I could just about make out an offshore wind farm, with rows of tall white wind turbines topped with blades spinning in unison in the afternoon drizzle. As we meandered through southern Sweden the train showed off its tilting capabilities as it gently leaned to one side and then the other as we cut through the increasingly undulating terrain. Up until now my journeys had been across largely flat land, but now hills were springing up on either side of the train, mostly covered in chunks of dense forest and patches of sharp grey rock, with the occasional smooth reflective surface of a lake mixed in as added contrast.

The carriage was relatively empty, and I had comfortably settled in to what was now becoming my train routine: taking off my shoes, slipping in my earphones and watching the miles whiz past through the window. The stops were few and far between, largely down to the minimal presence of any towns along the way. Sweden is a relatively sparsely populated country, with many of its inhabitants living in one of the two major cities: Gothenburg in the west of the country, or the capital, Stockholm, on the eastern side. It was the latter that was to be my next stop on my Euro trip.

Chapter 10

Stockholm, Sweden

It was gone seven as I stepped off the train. Outside the sky was an exciting combination of colours thanks to the sunset that was taking place behind a mottled variety of clouds. Some were high up cirrus affairs, with streaks of reds and oranges lightly sponged across the horizon, whilst others featured deep blues and menacing greys of the cumulonimbus variety, looming ominously overhead.

Having congratulated myself for that strong recital of GCSE meteorology, I turned my attention to the task of finding my accommodation for the night. Once again I had a small scribble on a page to guide me, and very quickly it proved itself inadequate. I took a gamble and turned right from the station and soon found water. This was excellent, as water featured prominently on my hand drawing. Unfortunately, having crossed over the river I found myself on what appeared to be a small island. It was a very nice island, with cobbles leading up to a large church with a dark framework spire. The gaps in the spire allowed the contrasting shades of light through, creating a very striking presence as it was silhouetted on the skyline. It looked strangely familiar, although certainly not from the scribble on the page I had held out in front of me. I then realised that I'd seen it before, albeit in a far more scaled down form. This was the focus of the scene depicted in the miniature representation of Stockholm I'd seen at *Mini Europe* in Brussels. It was slightly strange to now be stood in the middle of that scene – taking the place of the tiny model people - but it was nice to now see it in its original setting (and original size). However, the very existence of this seemingly deserted island in the heart of the city on which it stood very much went against my drawing. I would later discover that the city is actually set across 14 islands, and there's your quick nod to the benefits of prior research.

As I contemplated this new realisation that I had no real idea where I was, the aforementioned ominously dark cumulonimbus clouds decided to do what they had threatened. I ducked into a nearby shop doorway to seek shelter, rummaging in my backpack for some rain-defensive layering. I pulled out my jacket and slipped it on - zipping it up to the top and pulling over the hood to complete my weather-battle-ready attire. In some ways I was grateful for needing to use it, as so far it had been surplus to requirements thanks to the largely bright and sunny weather that you would expect with summer (queues for Dutch museums aside). After all, no one likes carrying around unnecessary luggage. It did however mean that I was now fighting the elements as well as the confusing geography of the Swedish capital.

After nearly an hour that included many bridge-crossings (often back and forth as I discovered further parts of the city that were interesting, but ultimately irrelevant to my search) I finally stepped onto a road that had a name I recognised. In some ways it was good that I'd been forced to check my hand written annotations so many times that the names were engraved in my memory, as the now persistent rain had soaked into the flimsy bit of paper and caused the ink to run, blurring the text into an incomprehensible black sludge. Darkness had now also well and truly set in, but luckily I noticed the hostel sign semi-hidden in a small, understated doorway halfway along the road. I was very relieved at having finally made my destination. Sadly this was short lived, as evidently my faffing about on all the bridges and pretty cobbled islands had caused me to miss check-in hours, and I now faced an awkward and slightly confusing out-of-hours entry system. I pressed a button on the neighbouring speaker panel, and after a short recorded message in Swedish, a gruff and muffled voice cut in. I politely explained my situation as raindrops trickled down my nose, and after a few seconds of deliberation from the person on the other end of the intercom, I was deemed worthy of entry. There was a buzz and I pushed open the heavy door and descended down a flight of stairs to a starkly lit reception area at the bottom. The place appeared to be deserted as I stood in the middle of the room, dripping on the tiled floor and trying to work out what the next step of locating my bed was. Thankfully I noticed the small envelope stuck on the closed reception shutter before I had made too much of a puddle. It had my name neatly hand-written on it, along with what I took to be my room number: 10. I peeled off the envelope – warmed by this personal touch - and opened it up. Inside I found a couple of slips of paper; one had a door code written on it, and the other a room plan with an 'X' marked on one of the beds. I now faced the next challenge: where was room 10? There was a corridor to my right that had rooms 2 to 9 leading off it. Then behind the staircase that led back up to street level was room 1. There appeared to be no room 10, though. I definitely felt like I was being punished for showing up late. I made two more pointless trips along the first corridor - just in case my powers of door number observation had failed me the first time – but to no avail. There was still no one about, and I was now dribbling a trail of water all around the hostel. I then noticed another door at the opposite end of the reception area that was numberless. I cautiously pushed on it with my cold, damp hand, and it creaked open gently like in a horror film. Behind it was a small kitchen and lounge area that was again void of any signs of life. I was just about to close the door again when I spotted another door at the far end of the room. I walked over to it and found a whole new complex of corridors and rooms beyond. Finally I found room 10, hidden in the far corner of this weird, empty underground hostel maze. I punched in the door code from the slip of paper and the lock clicked open satisfyingly. I was in. My bed was exactly where the room plan had prophesised, and I was even treated to another hand written note.

'We have provided linen for you in case you did not bring your own,' it read.

This was very kind of them, because they were right, I *hadn't* brought my own linen.

But it continued, 'this will be an extra 18 Krona charge.'

Oh. This was less welcome. I've never understood why some hostels charge extra for linen. I assume if you book a bed it will come with the necessary bed paraphernalia. When you make a reservation for a train they don't charge you for the seat fabric. I have also never met a backpacker who carries a full set of bed linen, and normally these hostels ban you from using sleeping bags or sleeping bag liners, so there's really no way around it.

I decided that I would have a shower. I was cold and wet from the rain, but also hot and irritated from the urban-trekking and linen charges. I unpacked my towel and found the washroom, and after dousing myself in pleasant warm water I was soon feeling refreshed. That was until I came to drying myself. The shower was operated by a fancy motion-sensor, and as I began to re-dress in the cubicle I discovered that the room's lighting was also motion-sensitive. I had obviously been too still in my showering because the lights suddenly all went out. I bashed my elbow on the door as I felt for the catch to open it. I lent out of the cubicle in my boxer shorts and flapped my arm, desperately trying to re-trigger the lights. Unfortunately my other arm went off in the other direction as a counter-balance, inadvertently triggering the shower sensor. The lights then flickered back on, brightly illuminating the washroom once again and highlighting my now soaked lower body, including underwear, as well as my jeans that had fallen off the door hook in the kafuffle. I cursed loudly. Sweden was not going well.

After a relatively disrupted night's sleep thanks to dodgy broken bed slats, I got up early to see if the city was ready to make amends for my pretty disastrous arrival the previous evening. I met a couple of English guys - Chris and Ed – in the kitchen, and after a brief chat we all set off together to explore Stockholm.

It was now clear blue skies as we cut down through a busy pedestrianised shopping area towards the centre of the city. We crossed over the water via Norrbro, which took us past Riksdagshuset; the Swedish parliament building that sits on its own little island between central Stockholm and Gamla Stan (the Old Town). We then found ourselves below the imposing facia of Kungliga Slottet - the Royal Palace. Up a cobbled ramp in front of the huge baroque building was an occupied guard post. Although not dressed in quite as striking attire as the classic British Beefeater, there was still something appealing as a tourist about the formal way he was stood outside his little box. Chris and Ed decided to walk up to him. Again unlike a Beefeater, this guard was evidently not under strict instructions to stare unwaveringly straight ahead, because as soon as Chris and Ed stepped over a barely noticeable semi-circular line of cobbles that were in subtle contrast to the otherwise horizontal rows, the guard made angry growling noises and pointed forcefully at their feet. Clearly this was his domain, and he was not going to let a group of carefree Brits infiltrate it. Chris and Ed stepped apologetically away, before positioning themselves on either side of the curve of cobbles as I took a picture. We decided against asking to try on his hat. To be honest it wasn't a very nice hat, anyway.

Having finished annoying the local military we decided to embark on what we hoped would be a less troublesome activity. As there was so much water around Stockholm I suggested that we took a trip out onto it in whatever water-based vessel we could find. The others happily agreed, and so we wandered off in search of something appropriate. There were a number of tourist cruise boats going up and down the canals and waterways, but they all looked a little tame and also quite expensive. I then noticed a 'water sports centre' on the map that I'd been carrying in my pocket. This sounded more exciting, and as it was apparently near a bridge not too much further on from where we were, we set off in search of it.

Upon arrival it appeared that 'water sports centre' might have been a slight exaggeration. It was actually a few pedal boats and a couple of up-turned kayaks dumped on a small patch of dirty brown sand with a small wooden hut next to it. But, undeterred, we approached the hut and enquired about taking one of the dubious looking crafts out on to the water. The man in the hut seemed impressively nonplussed by the potential of what appeared to be some much needed business, but he grudgingly agreed to take our money, before waving his arm in the general direction of the water.

'Where are we allowed to go?' I asked, aware that often these activities have strict areas where you can paddle about, and I feared if we breeched the specific boundaries we would come under fire from a miserable and highly territorial military guard. The man in the hut seemed less fussed than I'd imagined, however.

'Try to not go in the sea' he replied with a smirk.

The open sea was several kilometres away and around a lot of islands and inlets; it would be a quite remarkable feat to make it there and back in the hour we had paid for. I muttered a sarcastic 'tak', and then scowled at him as we clambered down onto the makeshift beach to put on lifejackets.

Once we had completed the slightly strenuous task of unhooking the kayaks and had dragged them into position, we clambered in and soon were happy paddling off across the calm waters. We headed out into a wide section of water that ran alongside a large area of parkland. There was no one else out on the water, and the tranquil setting was even more of a surprise given how close we were to the centre of the city. It was the high season, but the wide expanses of water and neighbouring greenery seemed to swallow up any people that were out and about on this summer's day, leaving the surroundings looking strangely deserted.

We paddled around for the next half an hour, setting our sights on various sections of the riverbank before approaching them and realising there wasn't much we could do once we got there, besides getting caught up in dense patches of reeds and other water-based shrubbery, meaning we had to jab away with our oars to escape them. We then spotted what looked like a raft floating in the middle of the water, but after an enthusiastic period of paddling, we discovered it was just a few planks of wood tied to a buoy. It was all a little tame, and we were starting to get a little bored of the peacefulness, so we turned around and paddled back towards the bridge where the 'water sports centre' was, and carried on past it in the other direction to where we had just come from. The water was narrower here, and there were also a lot of yachts moored on either side. We were entering the harbour area, where many of the tourist vessels that we had previously dismissed were now ploughing through the water on their way to various waterside attractions around the city. We soon realised that many of these routes included the stretch of water where we were now flapping about with our oars. It soon became very apparent that we had strayed into a busy shipping (or at least boating) lane.

Suddenly the water wasn't as calm anymore. The wash from all the boats criss-crossing ahead sent waves at our little kayaks in quick succession, knocking us around in all directions. We started bumping into each other, and then we were sent dangerously close to some rather expensive yachts that looked like the type owned by people who didn't appreciate kayak marks across their pristine hulls. We fought with the waves, trying our best to steady ourselves and avoid hitting things. A large tourist bus-boat then appeared from around a nearby inlet, powering through the water purposefully towards us. Some more frantic paddling ensued as we tried to escape the path of the on-coming boat. As we bundled into a set of buoys, the boat sounded its horn, threateningly. This seemed to trigger an impressive climatological event in which dark clouds suddenly drew together overhead and let rip on us. As the packed tourist boat thundered past, we waved as if we were part of a highly skilled and elaborate water-based entertainment act - designed to look like a group of hapless, uncoordinated kayakers put on especially for the passing passengers. Faces stared blankly back at us. A Chinese man took a photo, whilst a little girl frowned and waved a small flag. Once clear of any imminent danger, and with weary arms and increasingly damp clothing, we battled our way back to the shoreline. The man in the water sports hut was still apparently devoid of all personality, and he seemed indifferent to our watery plight as we dragged the flooded kayaks up the grubby sand and peeled off our sodden life jackets.

We were pretty drained as we pushed our way through the heavy wooden door of a restaurant in a narrow cobbled passage in Gamla Stan. The light, passing shower that we had anticipated had in fact turned into a heavy and persistent downpour. We were thoroughly soaked. My jacket had successfully demonstrated that vital difference between 'water resistant' and 'waterproof', and my jeans had doubled in weight with water saturation. My summery canvas shoes had also taken a weathery beating, and were now kindly highlighting all the seams that were open to water absorption. We took seats at a table under the highly dubious and watchful eyes of a smartly clad waiter and assessed the menu. Whilst the other two tried to decipher the text in the hope of choosing us an exciting local dish for us to try, I sneakily removed my soaked shoes and socks and pushed them under my seat. We had unwittingly chosen a table on the edge of a small mezzanine level, and as a result my grubby, damp feet were on display to diners on the lower level. I wasn't proud of this, but needs must, and I'm sure they just put it down to some odd cultural tradition from this group of strange 'out-of-towners' that had infiltrated what was increasingly (and slightly worryingly) revealing itself to be quite a classy establishment. I suddenly became aware of the gentle murmurings of classical music as the waiters glided around the floor carrying woven baskets of bread that were never left on the table long enough for you to properly sample. I noticed neat little bouquets of flowers that formed the main flourish of the centrepieces that sat in the middle of each table, and I was under no doubt that in a few hours candles would emerge to accompany them. I then turned my attention to the menu. There were some very high numbers next to each option that confirmed my suspicions: this place was *bloody expensive*.

Meatballs. *That's* what we ended asking for: *traditional Swedish* meatballs. We didn't see them mentioned on the menu but had noticed them marked on the chalkboard outside. We thought this was a good option, as not only did it satisfy our keenness to sample a local delicacy, but also, how expensive can meatballs be? While we waited to find out I gently squeezed my socks to expel some of the water. A little trickled towards the edge of the mezzanine, and fearing a small-scale waterfall splashing down on to an unassuming Swedish couple below, I quickly wiped it clear with my other foot. This knocked me back to square one, as I now had a wet foot again. Thankfully the food didn't take long to arrive and I was soon distracted from my damp situation. I was mostly distracted because I had never seen meatballs presented in such an unnecessarily pretentious manner. We sat in silence, our clothing lightly dripping on the solid oak floor. Before each of us were three meatballs sat neatly in a row along a rectangular plate. Each one was topped with a light coloured sauce and some bizarre looking greenery poking out of the top. I wiped a raindrop from my nose, lifted my fork and jabbed at one of the meatballs. I'm not sure what I was expecting – perhaps it to burst into a rendition of *Super Trooper*, although I was very glad that it didn't.

In no time at all our meatballs had been devoured. We tried to savour them as much as we could, but it was difficult given how hungry we were, and how little there was on the plate to begin with. Annoyingly they gave us little more than a quick swipe at the bread basket, and so soon we had nothing left to do but await the bill. This arrived in a suitably slick manner courtesy of one of the hovering waiters, who placed a classy leather bound book on the table. I cautiously opened the cover and peered inside. The raindrops that had been dripping onto the highly polished table quickly turned to tears. I won't be too specific (I did my best to block out the financial damage) but you could have probably had a reasonable pub meal for the price of each one of those meatballs. I re-attached my shoes and we swiftly exited – our stomachs only a little fuller, our wallets considerably emptier.

Thankfully the skies had cleared as we set off once again through the cobbled streets of Gamla Stan. Unfortunately the brief respite from the elements in the restaurant had done little to dry our clothes, and so as we made our way back to the hostel we stopped off at a Swedish institution: *H&M*. We had done well to avoid this native clothing outlet for as long as we had, seeing as how many of their logos and shop fascias we had passed today, but we now found ourselves in desperate need of emergency trousers. We had all been travelling light and so these sudden (and wholly unsummery) weather variations had thoroughly caught us out. Perhaps it was all a marketing ploy to make us buy Swedish goods, as if rinsing us in the restaurant hadn't been enough.

Half an hour later we were back at the hostel, now sporting what I assume were very fashionable (and pleasingly good value) Swedish leg-wear, we played cards and plotted some evening exploits. Chris had read that there was a free walking tour that he was keen to do, and slightly reluctantly I agreed to go along as well. At half past seven the three of us were stood in a large open square in the middle of Stockholm. There was a large and slightly odd shaped fountain at the far side, blasting water high into the warm evening air. As we hovered about wondering what the protocol was for the beginning of a free tour that started in a vaguely designated place, a youngish guy in a tracksuit top appeared beside a tree and raised a hand in an authoritative manner. Suddenly lots of people who had been subtly lurking around various corners of the square all descended on the tree in an instant. It was an impressive display, and one we had little choice but to join.

Now I'm not really a fan of guided tours. My enjoyment of travel stems from the freedom to do what I want, when I want. I'm also not too keen on explicitly touristy exploits, even if many of the places I visit and things I do are sometimes pretty obvious visitor attractions; I at least want to explore them on my own terms. The idea of spending a hefty chunk of my evening being led slowly around the city by an old man in ridiculous shorts as he points out 'significant' paving slabs and describes in frustrating detail the history of the local window-frame-making industry was therefore far from appealing. I also feared being dragged through this ordeal as part of a group of dreary 'older' holidaymakers, who would probably be wearing ill-fitting khaki shorts with guidebooks falling out of their brightly coloured waterproof jackets that they insist on wearing to demonstrate their climatological preparedness. Not to mention the large and expensive cameras that would inevitably be slung around their necks to demonstrate a perceived deep photographic knowledge, even though they have all the settings on 'automatic'. Then at the end of this 'free' tour we would have to hand over a ridiculous sum of money as a 'tip' for the pleasure of having wasted an evening filled with awkward and painful disappointment.

However, my incredibly strong and unjustified preconceptions of 'free walking tours' were shown to be completely unfounded. Michael - the charismatic part-time student, part-time city guide - whisked the large, youthful audience around the city centre and through the Old Town with infectious enthusiasm. The attentive and widely international group of followers clung to his descriptions of the places of interest we would pass, packing each of the brief pauses in the tour with interesting insights into local customs and intriguing historical anecdotes. These included tales of the city's economic importance and geographical placing in Scandinavia, which made Stockholm a target for conflict, with Danish King, Christian II's arrival in 1520 resulting in a massacre of local resistance known as the 'Stockholm Bloodbath'. On a lighter note we were also told about 'fika' – the Swedish term for meeting up with friends for a coffee and a catch-up. Apparently it's common to invite friends to 'fika' a few times a day during work. I'm not sure how this affects Swedish productivity, but judging by the city's prices it hasn't seemed to suffer. Perhaps all the caffeine means that when they do find time to get on with some work, they do it all hyped-up and in double-speed.

The hour-long tour whizzed by, and once we had wound our way through the narrow alleyways of Gamla Stan and arrived in darkness by the waterside we were all more than happy to thrust some notes and coins into Michael's hand in firm appreciation of his efforts. Having absorbed so much information in the time, we then felt in need of absorbing something else, so the three of us went off to 'fika' (except with beer instead of coffee).

Chapter 11

Oslo, Norway

I had to leave early the following morning, but as I packed up my bag I realised that I hadn't paid for the hostel (and bed sheets, of course). I then found out that the reception didn't open until nine o'clock. I decided to solve this issue in the manner in which it had started, and so I tucked the appropriate number of Krona into an envelope with a note, and dropped it under the reception shutter. Soon I was back on the platform at Copenhagen's main station in anticipation of my next trip on the rails of Europe: a five-hour journey heading west across central Sweden and over the border to the Norwegian capital, Oslo.

The train was comfortable, with another well-appointed carriage acting as my base from where I could watch all the logging exploits that were taking place across the Swedish countryside as part of an uneventful journey. Uneventful, aside from one unusual moment when a smartly attired lady who was sitting next to me and quietly eating a sandwich, suddenly lurched across my lap as I sat calmly looking out of the window. I found this dramatic surge of activity a little alarming, but I soon realised that she was reaching for a plastic waste bag from the dispenser that the train company had thoughtfully provided below the window. Her initial grab proved unsuccessful though, and soon she was just sprawled over my sitting space, clawing desperately at the bags as I sat back awkwardly trying to act like everything was normal. In the end I cautiously edged my hand up and tore off a bag for her. She took it and then retreated back to an upright position in her seat, looking quite flustered as her cheeks broke out in a vibrant red colour.

There were a number of things that seemed to mark the crossing of the border from Sweden to Norway. Firstly, the tree trunks got thinner. This might seem like a strange point to pick up on, but it made the trees look more elegant. However, on the downside I also assume this meant that they were less appealing to loggers, as the logging activity that had been so prolific earlier in the journey had now vanished. Secondly, the unreliable weather that had blighted my visit to Sweden gave way to clear blue skies. This had the effect of illuminating the many houses that increasingly appeared dotted about the lush green hills beside the train tracks, immaculate in appearance with their white-washed walls and vibrant red-tiled roofs. Crisp, tree-lined rivers now also emerged, swinging through the valleys and feeding lakes with alluring blue water that glistened in the afternoon sun. The final indication was a little more technical, as I noticed that all of the 'Os' were now struck-through on the station signs, making them 'Øs'. I was looking forward to getting out and exploring this third Scandinavian stop on my trip across the continent, and I sensed that our arrival was not far away. However, we made one last stop before reaching the train's final destination of Oslo, and it was here that an elderly Russian couple got on board and sat in the seats in front of me. The man immediately fell asleep against the window and began emitting the most horrific snoring noises I've ever heard. This rather tainted the otherwise very pleasant entry into Norway.

My first half an hour in Oslo was once again spent incorrectly interpreting the latest offering in my hand-scribbled map series. Thankfully I managed to get hold of a more reliable source of navigation from the station's information desk, and then it wasn't long before I was pushing myself through the door of a clean and empty dorm room. In my experience I've found that it's very unusual to have the luxury of being able choose from all the beds. More often than not I find you have to barge the door open, nudging various open suitcases and backpacks out of the way before stepping carefully over the clothing-shrapnel that has erupted from them. You then have to (sometimes hazardously in the dark) feel your way around until you find a spare bed, which is inevitably a top bunk at the far end of the bombsite of habitation. So to have the luxury of choice was a little daunting. I stood hesitantly in the middle of the room for a few seconds before eventually choosing a bottom bunk on the left hand wall. As I put my bag down beside the bed and dropped my map on the pillow to mark my territory, I heard the door open behind me. In struggled a smallish girl with wild red hair and thick-rimmed glasses. Towering over her was a giant backpack, that judging by the way she was swaying seemed to have the dominant say in her directional movements. She came to an awkward stop in the middle of the room and surveyed the scene, much as I had done a few seconds earlier. We exchanged hellos whilst she assessed her (slightly reduced) choice of beds. I noticed a Swiss flag sewn neatly onto her bag.

'Hmmm, I think I sleep on top of you' she finally announced after half a minute of careful consideration.

I quickly looked up from the map I'd been studying. This seemed quite forward given that we'd only met nine seconds ago, and with so many free beds it seemed a little unreasonable, too. She then placed her backpack at the foot of my bed, pulled out a few items and hoisted herself up on to the bunk above. I sighed in relief, glad that I wasn't sharing a room with a nutter. I then heard her rustling about on the creaky bed frame, tussling with bed sheets and belongings before she jumped down and scuttled off to the bathroom. I went back to looking at my fold out map of the city as I plotted my afternoon's explorations. After a couple of minutes of map-based musings I decided that I would wander down to the waterfront. I was about to get up and implement this master plan when I heard a soft thud behind me. I took a swift look around, and just as I was about to turn back to my map again I suddenly spotted a piece of lime green material subtly nestled between my pillow and the duvet. This was strange, because I was pretty sure that I didn't own any lime green material. I leaned over to investigate. It looked silky and had frilly edges. This was very peculiar, because I *definitely* don't own anything with frilly—

I heard the toilet flush and turned to face the bathroom door in horror. It had dawned on me: this was *her* clothing – the Swiss girl's! It must have fallen down the side of the bunk! I glanced back at the offending item. It suddenly became obvious that this was no ordinary piece of clothing, either - these were her *pyjamas*! I had a Swiss girl's silky green pyjamas on my bed! Not only that, but they were now nestled - yes, *nestled* - between my pillow and duvet! *How did this happen*?! How did they fall into such an awkward position?! Now I looked like the nutter! The type of nutter that takes a girl' s silky lime green pyjamas and tucks them between his pillow and duvet! But I'm not that type of a nutter! Or *any* type of a nutter for that matter! It was all a horrible accident of poorly placed pyjamaring on her part! The bathroom door then swung open, and I quickly turned to face her. Thankfully my sitting position blocked the terrible sight behind. I had to think fast. There was *no way* I could let her see what had happened. She would see her silky lime green pyjamas nestled between my pillow and duvet and start panicking, which to be honest would be a bit rich given how she had propositioned me after nine seconds, but I knew that would never hold up in court.

'Is the window open? It's quite cold in here' I quickly asked, probably sounding a little exasperated due to my exasperation.

It wasn't cold; it was over 20 degrees and the middle of summer.

She looked at me a bit oddly (although with wild red hair and thick-rimmed glasses any look she gave looked a bit odd) and then wandered over to the window on the other side of the room to inspect it. As soon as her back was turned I quickly swung around, grabbed the pyjamas and whipped them back up on to her bed. I then sat down again, completing the delicate manoeuvre in one swift action.

She tapped at the window, scratched her giant mop of red hair and turned back around, giving me a shrug as she did so. I smiled, then grabbed my map and hurried out of the door. I never want to be first in a hostel dorm room ever again.

I strolled along the busy pedestrianised Karl Johans Gate, with its many shops that were sucking in and spilling out locals and visitors alike along the wide and cluttered paving. The street was also playing host to a number of artists and performers that were entertaining large, drifting crowds as they showed off their niche skills and artistic abilities. A man in a battered leather jacket scribbled away on the paving slabs with a worn-down piece of chalk as he depicted a colourful interpretation of a shooting star, whilst a man and woman performed a bizarre theatrical performance in the centre of the street beside a caravan as part of what appeared to be some form of protest or awareness campaign. I weaved through the throngs of shoppers and on past the parliament building towards Palace Park and its centrepiece, the Royal Palace. People were scattered across the grass; picnicking, chatting or quietly reading beneath the sun's rays. Behind the palace I found two mini lakes that were edged with people feeding ducks or sheltering from the sun under the clusters of trees. I carried on and ended up down by the rather ugly looking City Hall. Despite the fiercely geometric blocks of the brick exterior, the inside hosts an impressive array of vibrant artwork across the walls of the expansive main hall. I didn't stay long though, as the scene through the windows on the other side drew me back out into the sun. I came out onto a busy promenade alongside the harbour, where little tourist boats were ducking in and out of docking stations as they picked up passengers in between voyages out around the neighbouring fjordal inlets. I headed along one side of the harbour area, which took me right up alongside a giant cruise ship. I wasn't sure if it was the one I'd seen in Copenhagen, and I had no intention of sticking around to investigate. Instead I climbed up a small hill to a low-key fortification that sat adjacent to the imposing presence of the ship, and disappeared behind its stone walls.

There was a pleasant breeze rolling off the fjord as I found my way back to the waterfront near the main train station. The afternoon air was cooling and the sun was now balanced on the horizon as the evening drew in. It was perhaps the perfect light to first catch sight of the Operahuset – the home of Norwegian opera and ballet. Opened in 2008, this striking piece of architecture was designed to look like an iceberg, and with its sharp, angular roof sections and white granite and glass surfaces it does a pretty good job of it. The best part of this novel design is that you can walk up it, with the sloped roof sections leading to the top of the building, from where you're treated to impressive panoramic views across the city and out over the deep blue waters of Oslofjord. The waterfront is clearly an area on the up, with a row of tall, shiny glass-clad buildings in their latter stages of construction rising up from beside a busy highway. I sat up on the wall of the roof and looked out at the calm waters, the breeze carrying the intermittent sound of music to my ears. It wasn't the atmospheric melodies of an operatic soprano from the auditoriums below, however, but the thrashing sounds of a heavily distorted guitar and the deep, stomach-pounding thud of a bass drum. I looked across, and in the middle distance I could see the unmistakable form of a stage, with bright lights flashing across colourful swathes of people. A music festival was clearly in full flow a little further around the fjord, in what was undoubtedly a novel setting beside the water.

Directly below my dangling feet I had a birds eye view of those strolling about outside of the Opera House. There were even a couple of people who appeared to be pointing up towards me, including a man with a dark hat and matching uniform. He then started walking hurriedly towards the side of the building. I decided that perhaps I had flaunted the relaxed wandering policies of the roof system a little too much, and so I quickly jumped down from the wall and made my way back down to the entrance, narrowly avoiding the security guard as he went around the other way. I took a quick look inside the equally impressive foyer of the building, but soon realised that within the oak panelled atrium I was a little out of place in my jeans and t-shirt. Everyone else was in sparkly dresses or shirts and ties, gearing up for the evening's performance. I decided to leave on my own accord before I was politely removed.

As I meandered back towards the hostel I noticed a number of tables and chairs scattered out across a paved square. They were largely occupied with people sipping beverages or tucking into food. I realised that I was quite thirsty from my afternoon excursions, and so I found the neighbouring building that supplied these refreshments and ordered a beer. The barman duly obliged, and soon I was clutching a glass tankard. I handed over some notes and then took my beer outside and found a table. Once seated I opened my hand to put the change back into my wallet, but paused as I looked at the coins. There were far less there than I had expected. I did a quick calculation and realised that this beer had cost me the best part of eight pounds. I think I shed a tear as I tipped the glass slowly against my lips, vowing to savour every sip. This costly purchase coincided with a sudden drop in air temperature as evening firmly set in, and as the realisation of what a night out in Oslo must cost sent further shivers down my spine, I decided to have an early night.

The following morning, having thankfully avoided any Swiss interventions during the night, I set off towards the Botanical Gardens. It was a pleasant summer's stroll through the deserted pathways that weaved around trees and flowerbeds full of various planting and shrubbery I have no knowledge about. This was okay though, as I wasn't on a horticultural mission of discovery; I was in art mode.

The Munch Museet is, as you may well expect, a museum dedicated to the work of the famous Norwegian artist, Edvard Munch. The expressionist painter is best known for *The Scream*, which depicts a person holding their face in a horrified manner on a bridge below a vibrant sky. There are four versions of the picture, and the Munch Museum holds one of the painted versions. The painting was actually stolen in 2004, along with another of his pieces, *Madonna*, but thankfully both were recovered in 2006, which was handy, as I wanted to have a look at them today.

Stepping through the entrance it became clear that I was not alone in seeing this particular piece as the main draw (excuse the pun) of the museum. Although quiet at this early morning hour, the gift shop that fills the vast majority of the entrance foyer was full of *Scream* related offerings. T-shirts, pencils, bags, posters and keyrings all bore the iconic image, which was a bit annoying really, because their prevalence made them unavoidable as I made my way from the ticket desk and through the security scanner arch, and threatened to take the shine off seeing the original. Once through the checks, the first room gave a timeline history of Munch; from regular illness and the death of his mother when he was young, to the difficult and oppressive upbringing he faced from his father, as well as the turbulent times he experienced whilst pursuing his art. After all the gift shop gimmickry and having done a fair amount of reading I was then keen to start actually *seeing* some of his art, and so I headed down a long corridor until I entered a room that to my great relief contained some paintings. There was no gentle introduction though, as the artwork I found was striking to put it mildly, and certainly suggested that a complex mind was behind it. The translation revealed that I was in the *Puberty* exhibition. All the paintings featured naked people looking haunted. Vibrant colours and swirling backgrounds made for a compelling but also quite disturbing collection. I cautiously approached some of the paintings and tilted my head sideways like I've seen people do on television when they want to show that they are deeply engaged with a piece of artwork and they are using this new perspective to gain further insight into the mind of the artist. I just found this made my neck ache and the descriptions harder to read.

After three rooms and connecting corridors of works in this style and theme I felt that I'd seen enough expressionist puberty for one morning, and I was ready to see the main piece that brings people here. Instead, though, I found a turnstile and an exit door. I was puzzled. I was pretty sure that I hadn't seen *The Scream* in the exhibition, and I'm sure I would have recognised it from all the *Scream*-based paraphernalia I had seen in the entrance foyer. I cheekily squeezed back through the turnstile and began retracing my steps through the swirling imagery, closely checking the descriptions in case I had misunderstood what the pictures were.

Whilst the subjects in the paintings all looked quite tortured, I was sure none of them were screaming.

Eventually I found myself back in the first room from where I had entered the exhibition, and it was here that I noticed a small, unmarked doorway in the corner that I'd missed before. I wandered over and peered inside. Here I found a small huddle of people all crowded around a set of three paintings, and through a gap I could just about make out that the picture on the left was *The Scream*. I was pleased to have found it, but also slightly baffled that it hadn't been given more prominence or even signposting in the gallery. It would be very easy to miss, as I had aptly demonstrated whilst I was going through *Puberty*. As with many famous paintings though, it was a bit of an anti-climax. The fact that it wasn't the centrepiece seemed strange, but it does appear to be part of a set, and the smallest one at that. Ultimately though, it's an intriguing painting that has similar qualities (unsurprisingly) to many of Munch's pieces: colourful, swirly and a little sinister. I was grateful that the figure in *The Scream* was clothed after what I had just witnessed next door, though. I managed to grab a few seconds of clear sight in which to marvel at the famous swirling sky and iconic face-clutching expression, just before a Chinese man showed complete disregard for all the other people gathered in the room as he stood right in front of it – blocking everyone's view whilst he tried his best (which for the record wasn't very good) to imitate the figure in the picture. I wondered if he'd recently arrived here from Brussels. I sighed, and then made my way back to the exit turnstile. I had planned on getting something to eat after visiting the gallery, but strangely Edvard's paintings had left me with no real desire to munch on anything for the time being. Instead I returned to my hostel, where I picked up my backpack and set off for the station. But not the *train* station this time; I was heading for the *bus* station, and as far as my train adventure was concerned it was about to get a lot more controversial, too.

Chapter 12

Oslo to Berlin

The traffic was bad. I'd forgotten how inconvenient travelling by road could be. The weather had aptly changed to be dull and dreary, and the stop-start nature of the journey was far from relaxing thanks to the old and decrepit bus I was travelling on. There were no wide, padded armrests and certainly no neat little waste bag dispensers beneath the window (although on second thoughts perhaps that wasn't such a bad thing). It was a 60 kilometre journey south from Oslo to my destination; Moss, or more specifically, Rygge Airport, just outside of Moss. Yes, there it is, I said it - that dirty word: *airport*. There was no special train service going from this airport either, I was here for the purpose of boarding a plane and flying.

Now, if you've been paying attention throughout this book so far, you will probably be shaking your head and sighing resignedly.

'Surely the whole point of this journey was to avoid flying and all its pitfalls and irritations?' you'll be saying. 'You've been so outspoken about how frustrating and disconnecting it is to fly between destinations and banging on about the brilliance and freedom of train travel!'

Well yes, this is very true, and I'd like to congratulate you on being so moral and faithful to the cause, but before you judge me too heavily, let me explain.

Yes, this journey *is* extensively about train travel (how else could I justify such a witty title?), but as previously mentioned I was also working to a very tight time scale. I had also backed myself into a geographical corner by visiting Norway, and the only way to get back heading across the continent would be to retrace my tracks through Sweden and Denmark, which would be very time consuming, not to mention how it would use up some precious journey allowances on my InterRail pass. So there it is. I was set to take a brief respite from the rails of Europe, but rest assured I would soon be back on track. Or *tracks*.

I had prepared for such eventualities by travelling light. One of the biggest pitfalls of budget air travel is the cost of check-in luggage, but I wasn't going to be caught out! I'd been very efficient and packed all my belongings for this trip into a bag that fitted the regulation cabin bag size allowance. My preparation spanned to other areas, too: I carried my toiletries in a clear, re-sealable bag, and all its contents were less than 100 millilitres. I was a pro. I had also pre-checked-in online as requested, and printed out my boarding pass. I even took off my belt *before* being asked to at the security check, and after a bit of a faff unlooping it from my jeans, I successfully managed to waddle through the metal detector arch without setting it off, and more importantly, without my jeans falling down. I really am the perfect air passenger.

I very quickly got bored of waiting at the departure gate. The luxury of train travel means that you don't have to show up hours in advance before you leave (or travel for an hour before you even get to your departure point). I wandered aimlessly around the sparse, uninspiring terminal building as I did my best to kill some time. I considered buying a bottle of water, but then decided not to, which pretty much sums up how dull my time there had become. I was briefly entertained by a conversation between two English guys ahead of me in the queue at the passport checking booth, who were having a very frank and in-depth discussion about *Marmite*. After spending a few minutes listing the various merits and drawbacks, they eventually concluded that 'you probably either love it...or you hate it.' I reckon they should go into marketing.

As I made my way back to the small amount of seating next to the gate, I noticed the metal stand that represents the allowed size of a cabin bag. I smiled, and then quickly stopped and frowned as I read the numbers: 55cm x 40cm x 20cm. I thought back to the slightly nerdy outing to the camping shop I had been on prior to my trip, where I had taken with me a measuring tape and had spent a good half an hour carefully measuring all the bags. I'd found a bag that fitted the strict cabin baggage measurements *perfectly*. It was *exactly* 56cm high, which is *exactly* the allowed height of what I suddenly now realised was a rival airline's cabin baggage allowance. I couldn't believe it. Why don't they standardise sizes across airlines?! This was a terrible development, because this now meant that my bag was one centimetre too high, or more worryingly, I potentially had an *extra 800* cubic centimetres too much baggage! This was very bad news indeed. All that strategic planning and it had all been ruined in an instant. I now had to be very cunning.

With nearly an hour still to go before our scheduled departure time people began queuing up at the gate. I never understood the need to queue so early, but now with my illegal cabin bag I needed to blend in with the crowd, and so I got up and joined them. After 20 minutes a lady wearing a bright blue outfit and far too much make-up began the arduous process of checking everyone's scrap of paper, or 'boarding pass' as they like to call it. I took this as my signal to suddenly realise that I was very cold, and so I pulled out my jumper *and* jacket from my bag and put them on, despite it being the middle of summer and very hot in the glass, greenhouse-like terminal building. In that instant I also realised that the book I had been reading was a real-page turner (even though I had successfully managed to avoid turning any of its pages for the past few days), and so I took that out of my bag and started reading it intently. Of course I needed a musical accompaniment to add to the literary drama, so out came my mp3 player, and I slotted the earphones into my ears. I also cleverly thought to pull out my camera, just in case I spotted an unusual Norwegian animal on the short walk across the tarmac to the aeroplane. Then I remembered that no flight boarding was complete without having toiletries in your jacket pocket, or a couple of pairs of socks stuffed into your armpits. Miraculously my bag suddenly seemed a little emptier, and after slinging it onto my back (and out of sight of the airline staff) I looked positively inconspicuous as my bulging, media-absorbed, over-dressed form shuffled along the queue. Once at the front I quickly handed over my ticket and hurried out towards the plane.

Once aboard I found a seat and quickly decanted into it. I gathered up my mix of belongings and re-packed them into my bag, before shoving it under the seat in front. I then removed my shoes to air my feet as is customary when I'm faced with sustained periods of travel, and soon I had next to no legroom at my disposal. The hot, sticky plastic-covered seating and stupidly bright headrest pressed up in my face confounded the level of discomfort I was set to travel in for the next couple of hours. I missed trains. Further flight-based misery followed as a young child's face emerged above the ad-filled headrest in front. Whilst simultaneously smiling and dribbling, the small boy started banging his little arms against the seat. This somehow dislodged a small river of empty chocolate wrappers and crisp packets that had been wedged between the seat and the fuselage, which now fell out and scattered across my minimal leg area. I was now cramped, being watched, and rustling with every restricted movement I attempted to make. Now I just had to wait for a sudden bout of turbulence to knock me unconscious against the window panel, so that the boy could draw a crayon moustache on me and throw up in my lap. I think I would have been better off in the hold.

'Good afternoon ladies and gentlemen, this is your captain speaking. I'm afraid we are waiting for some lost passengers, and so our departure will be delayed.'

Brilliant.

Shortly after this joyous announcement, a large sweaty man bumbled down the aisle and kindly wedged himself ungraciously into the seat beside me, his semi-viscous limbs spilling over the armrest and pressing up against me. He had been balancing an unnecessarily large stack of magazines as he wriggled into place, but now it all became too much for him and he spilt them over me. I helped collect them up and then turned sulkily to face the window. Eventually we took off, and the airline's challenge to try and flog the penned-in audience as much crap as possible in one hour commenced.

'Scratchcards?…Cigarettes?….Vodka?' came the shrill, piercing tones of the cosmetically-enhanced air stewardess. She stopped short of offering fireworks and pornography though, which really would have completed the debauched nature of mid-air consumerism. I put my earphones in and tried to lose myself in the thudding beat of some 90s Brit Pop.

After an uncomfortable hour or so, the pilot began carefully lining up the plane for landing, before slamming it as hard as he could into the tarmac to ensure everyone was awake. Despite his attempts to fracture the bones of all on board, as soon as we came to a standstill everyone jumped up from their seats and began throwing luggage around the cabin in the mass hysteria that accompanies a flight arrival. Overhead compartments were flung open and bag straps and suitcase handles became entangled with each other as frantic passengers desperately yanked at them. I remained in my seat, aware of the fruitlessness of trying to make a swift escape through the single exit at the front of the plane. I calmly waited for the bustle to die down before slipping out of my row and heading down to the exit unmolested.

'Some people are so fucking rude!' exclaimed the indignant air hostess after the man in front of me had failed to say goodbye to her. Maybe she needed to slap on another layer of make-up. That would probably get her the respect she craved.

Chapter 13

Berlin, Germany

People always speak highly of Berlin. Whether it's history buffs getting to grips with post-war division or party-animals seeking out a techno-filled warehouse rave – Berlin has something for everyone. Or at least everyone who fits neatly into these two quite specific categories. My interests are arguably a little broader. I was certainly intrigued by Berlin's historical significance, and I was keen to sample the contemporary musical offerings of the city, but I also wanted to go up a tower and eat some sauerkraut. Thankfully Berlin caters for this too.

I took the train from the airport into the city, getting off at Alexanderplatz, from where it was a short walk to my centrally-located hostel. Inside I was greeted by a rowdy bar scene, with groups of youthful travellers dotted around the many tables. Large flat screen televisions were showing various obscure sports from across the world, whilst film posters and sporting memorabilia hung from the walls and ceiling. This was the quintessential backpackers' hangout. I checked-in and headed up to my room where I met fellow Brits, Rob and Geoff, and with all of us having little planned for the day, we set off to explore.

We began our explorations by getting on a train from Alexanderplatz as we all had day passes for the city's rail network. On a map at the station we noticed a place to the west of the city called Spandau. Perhaps vague name associations with 80s pop acts isn't a particularly logical method for deciding on travel destinations, but our novel approach was rewarded as after a 20 minute journey to the end of the line we came across a fortress. Spandau Citadel is quietly nestled in this leafy Berlin suburb on a small island on the edge of the River Spree. It is – according to the leaflet that came with our three Euro entry ticket - one of the finest preserved renaissance military structures in Europe. I'll be honest, I've not got a particularly detailed knowledge of Europe's renaissance military structures, but this one was certainly very pleasant, and in the warm sunshine it was nice to wander around its near-deserted grounds. Inside there was a little museum, which told of its history since it was built in the 16th Century. Most recently it was used to house Prussian prisoners from the East, sitting as it did in the British sector of Berlin before reunification in 1989. From the museum we followed a series of spiralling wooden steps that led up to a roof top platform from where we were treated to clear views back across central Berlin. A gentle breeze lapped at a crest-laden flag hanging off one of the turrets, and as I scanned the horizon I immediately spotted the fort's more modern tower counterpart – the skyward-reaching TV tower – and mentally marked it as a destination for later in my visit.

On our way back to the station at Spandau we passed two more things of interest, the first being a set of traffic lights featuring the 'Ampelmann'. These pedestrian signals have a bit of cult-like status in their native Berlin. They initially look similar to regular red and green men used to indicate when you should cross a road that you might find anywhere, but then you notice that these men have hats, and their arms and legs appear joined without any defined torso. They were devised by physiologist Karl Peglau and introduced in the early 1960s as an accompaniment to vehicle signals to minimise traffic accidents. Apparently it was found that people react better to appealing symbols. If anything though, their intriguing appearance nearly had the opposite effect as I strayed hazardously between traffic islands, briefly mesmerised by their unusual form. The second thing that caught our attention was a poster stuck to one of the signal posts. It highlighted a football match between the local team, Hertha Berlin, and Italian *Serie A* giants, Juventus. We worked out that the match was today, and kicking off in less than an hour. After checking our map we discovered that the Olympic Stadium – the venue for the 2006 World Cup final and home to Hertha Berlin – was on the train line back to the city centre. Opportunism had struck.

Half an hour later and we were sat in the vast stadium, having picked up tickets on the gate for 15 Euros each. I'm a keen football fan, and I'd actually seen Hertha play 12 years ago on a visit to Munich, but this was Geoff's first ever football match. Despite the scale of the Olympic Stadium venue and the world-renowned footballing prowess of the visiting team, he looked impressively non-plussed by the occasion. Although this was a pre-season friendly, the half of the stadium that was open was packed, and we were surrounded by lots of enthusiastically rowdy Berlin fans. Banners, flags and intense chanting accompanied a half of relatively disappointing football that ultimately saw Juventus take a slender 1-0 lead. The crowd didn't seem overly bothered by this, though, and happily continued with their partisan serenades. At half time we headed out behind the stand, and having seen others do the same we purchased giant jugs of beer. This felt very German. We took them out onto the grassy banks that surround the stadium and laid down in the sun, lazily listening to the second half whilst occasionally glancing through the large gap at one end of the giant bowl-shaped arena to keep track of the score in between gulps of beer. We think the game finished 2-0 to Juventus, but in all honesty, with the amount of beer we'd consumed by the end courtesy of the massive jugs, it was difficult to be certain.

Berlin, Germany

By the time we got back to the hostel it was deep into the evening, and with very little persuasion needed we headed to the bar, where we conveniently discovered it was the early stages of 'happy-hour', or in this case, 'happy three-hours' – offering 2 for 1 on bottled beers. This was a welcome discovery, especially after the horrific cost of beer in Oslo. We placed our orders, found an empty table, and settled in for the evening.

It was the label on my shorts that first got my attention as I lay in bed the following morning. It took me a while to work it out, but I finally realised that there shouldn't have been a label sticking out of the front of the waistband of my shorts. It might be an unusual point to raise, but in that moment I found it deeply concerning. Labels should be at the back - they have no place at the front. It slowly occurred to me that I must have put them on back-to-front. I hadn't made an error like this since my childhood, and at 25 years old this was certainly not something I wanted to brag about. I tried to work out how this had happened, but quickly realised that I had very little recollection of anything that had happened in the previous nine hours, and putting on a pair of shorts was certainly not a stand-out moment. The only thing I could even loosely recall was a dream I'd had about being on a beach.

'Morning! Good beach party, wasn't it?' came a voice to my right. I peered cautiously through the wooden slats of my top bunk and saw Rob's face smiling inanely back at me.

How did he know about my dream? We had only met yesterday - he had no right to be prying into my dreams so early in our acquaintance!

And then I noticed he was holding a camera, and displayed on the little screen I could just about make out a picture of myself, sitting in sand and holding a beer. All of my clothes appeared to on the right way round (which was of some relief), but it still didn't make a lot of sense as Berlin is very much inland. There was a parasol in the picture too, and a girl who looked like she was talking to me. This was all very odd.

I got up, showered and then headed down to breakfast with Rob and Geoff, where we pieced together the evening over burnt toast and warm orange juice. Apparently we had got chatting to some Irish people in the hostel bar, who had at some point led us off into the night to a popular non-coastal beach resort where we had wilfully embraced the trendy beats of German minimalist techno until the early hours.

Still slightly confused, but thankfully now correctly dressed, I set off with the others to sample some of the more traditional offerings of Berlin. Our first stop was Checkpoint Charlie – one of the infamous crossing points of the Berlin Wall between East and West Berlin during the Cold War. A small outdoor museum over the road from the reconstructed hut offered a detailed account of the checkpoint's history of restricting access through the Soviet-built wall that was designed to stop residents of the Eastern bloc escaping to the West. A timeline of text and images highlighted some of the key instances where people had tried to make a break across the divide; through hiding in the back of cars, digging holes under the cover of darkness, or simply making more-or-less a run and jump for it. As the pictures graphically demonstrated, this often ended badly. Brightly decorated segments of the wall have been placed around the area as ad-hoc installations to bring an artistic flourish to a dark period in the city's past, and for a few Euros you can stand outside the hut next to a mock uniform-clad border control guard who will give you a hat to wear as you pose for a photograph next to him. As classy and culturally sensitive an opportunity as this was, we decided we wouldn't participate, and instead we set off to our next stop of our self-made tour – the Reichstag.

Home to the German parliament - or Bundestag - since 1999, this impressively renovated building used to house the Imperial Diet (or Reichstag) before a fire damaged it in 1933. The post-war divided Germany left the building unused and ignored until a newly unified nation had it restored in the early 1990s to eventually re-house the German parliament. It now has a very large glass dome protruding from the roof, and it's from within its winding ramps that an audio guide teaches you about the complex political structure and history as you make your way to the top. It also provides an overview of many of the other buildings and monuments you can see from the 360 degree viewing area, although as I discovered, if you didn't stop in the right place you risked getting a very confusing insight into the various buildings around the city. The skyline from this striking viewpoint becomes even more compelling when you hear about all the changes that Berlin has experienced (both physical and political). After hearing about the changing political balance across the country, as well as some of the significant decisions that have been tackled at the Reichstag over the last century, I considered raising the issue of my inconveniently delayed train from Duisburg to Hamburg with some senior political figures. Rob and Geoff seemed less concerned by my petty train-based frustrations, though (I suppose that's what you get when you fly everywhere), and luckily for them it appeared that parliament had broken up for the summer holidays, anyway.

By the time we had spiralled back down from the glass dome of the Reichstag it was late afternoon, and we were getting a little tired. We'd had a late night spent on the beach after all, and with the in-depth history lessons we'd been getting we were in need of a break. We took a quick detour through the Brandenburg Gate (passing further opportunities to dress up as soldiers that we politely declined) and headed back to Alexanderplatz. As we neared the hostel some ominously dark clouds ventured across the sky, and soon they were depositing their damp contents on us with some ferocity. We took shelter under the overhang of a building, where I found myself staring at a poster that intrigued me. It was advertising 'Buster Keaton Season'.

My dad loves telling my brother and me (and sometimes strangers when there's the slightest hint of justifiable relevance) about the time he played us a Buster Keaton film. I must have been about five years old, and my dad said he was going to put on a video (yes, again, please remember that this was the early 90s). He then told us that it was a silent film and that it was in black and white. My elder sibling and myself were less than impressed by this news, being very much fans of noisy colourful films as many young children are. Still, we sat there obediently, but probably sulking as the strange cinematic events took place before us on our mock-wooden-housed 4:3 aspect ratio television set. It is with great glee that my dad will then announce how by the end of the film the two of us were rolling about in fits of hysterics. One particular stand out moment I seem to recall is when Buster comes out of a building and gets into a car parked beside the kerb, which then does a swift U-turn and then he climbs out again on the other side of the road and goes into the building opposite. Comedy genius.

And here I was twenty-something years later, hiding from torrential rain in a dark side road of the German capital and once again looking at this rather niche, cult figure from my quite frankly poor film-watching history. It felt like there could be an opportunity here that was worth perusing. Ducking around the corner as we tried to avoid the persistent rain we found the entrance. This was an 'art cinema', and inside we found the foyer – with its elegant interior - was almost deserted. There was a showing starting in 10 minutes of Buster Keaton's *The General* – a perfect fit given my trip, as this is one of his better-known films about him scrambling about on a train. We bought three tickets, as well as a beer each and some popcorn before heading through to the auditorium. Rows of plush turquoise seating greeted us, which were all facing a stage where velvet curtains hung from the back and side walls. There were only a handful of other people waiting for the film to start, but no sooner had we chosen our seats then the lights dimmed and the curtains drew to reveal a very large screen. This shouldn't have come as a massive surprise – this was a cinema after all – but as I previously alluded to, my cinematic history is less than impressive. In fact I hadn't been to the cinema in nearly three years, and as a result I found the large visuals that were now flickering across the screen in front of me at a rapid rate a little daunting. Thankfully the beer took the edge off, although the irritating rustling and soft, squeaky texture of the popcorn reminded me of one of the reasons why I hadn't been in this environment for so long.

The film began, with the familiar grainy black and white film skipping along to the sharp, slapstick comedy antics of Buster Keaton as he gives chase to a stolen locomotive. As we sat back in the dry and comfortable surrounds of the cinema whilst Buster tumbled entertainingly around the screen, I became aware of the musical soundtrack that was playing over the film. In a surprise twist to this viewing I suddenly realised that it was being accompanied by live music. Sat at the front to the right of the stage was a grand piano, where a petite lady sat with her fingers briskly rippling over the keys. It was an unusual sight, and I assume this isn't a usual feature of cinema that has been introduced in my absence, but it was very enjoyable none-the-less. I recognised the style of the quick, light-touch piano playing that often featured in silent films of this era, but it was only after about 20 minutes that I realised she was playing melodic variations of *America* from *West Side Story*. I was bemused by this choice of music, not least because of its 1950s message: singing the praises of the US (albeit in a Latin American style) whilst being used here as the soundtrack to a 1920s film about conflict in the American Civil War. Perhaps the irony was intentional, or maybe the original sheet music had been damaged in the heavy rain on the way to the showing and she'd had to improvise. Whatever the motivation behind the choice of music, it was a remarkable feat of endurance that she kept playing continuously for the entire duration of the hour-or-so long film.

Back outside the rain had stopped and the clouds had vanished. It was heading rapidly towards dusk, but having successfully recovered in the calming surrounds of the art cinema we had one last tourist assignment to complete. The Fernsehturm (television tower) that I had admired from the top of the fort in Spandau was conveniently located near to our hostel, and it had proved to be a very useful homing landmark last night (or so I had been informed this morning). It is Germany's tallest structure, and at 368 metres it certainly dominates the skyline with its golf-ball-like sphere topped with a giant red and white antenna. We purchased tickets from its base, but because of its popularity we had half an hour before our allotted visiting time and so we headed over to nearby Alexanderplatz. Here we found a lively scene consisting of a selection of pop-up rides and performances that were taking place in between stalls selling a variety of cuisine. We walked around the busy square and then ate some bratwurst and sauerkraut next to The Weltzeituhr (World Clock) – a confusing cylindrical display of rotating rings and numbers that apparently tells the time in lots of different countries. As we stood munching on our sausages and chewing the vinegar soaked cabbage, the intricate workings of the clock left us none the wiser as to what time it was anywhere in the world, but it did occupy us until we could ascend the tower.

By the time we had queued and gone up in the lift to the viewing area it was almost dark. The panorama of lights spread out in all directions and off into the distance, with the silhouette of tall socialist tower blocks in the east of the city contrasting with the lower rise suburban housing to the west. The centre is a mix of historical buildings, modern art galleries and office blocks, with many shimmering in the reflection of the river Spree as it winds through the city. From here Berlin's divided history was even more marked. Of all the places I'd visited on this trip so far, this certainly felt like one that I could easily see myself coming back to, as there's so much to take in and explore. However I had to keep a close eye on my schedule, so we headed back to the hostel for a relatively early night – this time avoiding any beach excursions.

There was one more key stop I wanted to make before leaving Berlin, and so I got up early the following morning and headed out to the east of the city. Following on from yesterday's introduction to Berlin's infamous divide, we had learnt that the largest remaining section of the Berlin Wall formed what is now known as the East Side Gallery; a kilometre-long stretch of the ominous stone wall segments along Mühlenstraße that have been painted by artists from across the world following reunification in 1990. The paintings are a vivid display of bright colours and abstract imagery, with many, unsurprisingly, featuring themes of peace and unity. The striking flash of colour along the road masks the original border of the river Spree on its western side, whilst it faces out onto rather drab industrial looking areas beyond the nearby railway line. Despite 23 years having passed since the wall became redundant from its original purpose, there is still plenty of opportunity for this area to benefit from some urban regeneration. Not that there aren't signs that this is happening, as the nearby shiny glass structure of the *O2 World* arena aptly demonstrates.

Having walked the length of the East Side Gallery, observing the concrete canvases and trying to comprehend the often obscure metaphors and symbolism of the art work (as well as the less philosophical pen-markings – mainly in the 'Dave woz 'ere' vain) it was time to return to Alexanderplatz, ready to once more board a train as I continued east across the continent.

Chapter 14

Prague, Czech Republic

There was a marked shift on this train journey, because no longer was I sat in an open carriage, but for the first time on this trip I found myself in a train carriage with compartments. I did the uncomfortable thing that such set-ups require and bustled along the corridor, peering through the glass of each compartment to find one with space. I eventually chose the last one at the end of the carriage, so I had little alternative unless I wanted to lose face and head back past the others I'd already rejected. The compartment had a plumpish middle-aged man slumped semi-conscious against the window on one side, and a small, smartly dressed lady of a similar age sat opposite him. I softly slid open the door, smiled at the lady by way of a greeting and sat down quietly on one of the empty seats.

The journey passed in relative silence, aside from the intermittent sleep-mutterings of the man by the window and the occasional sliding of the compartment door back and forth. This happened every time a newly boarded passenger failed to adequately inspect the compartment by leering through the grubby window, and so they would stick their head through the door before considering the space, and then lean back out and quickly slam-slide the door closed again as an abrupt sign that they had chosen not to join us. The social pressures and the potential paranoia-inducing implications of this design of carriage must surely be the reason why they are no longer used on many train networks. Thankfully the socially pressured journey didn't drag on too much, and the suburbs of the Czech capital were soon visible through the murky window.

In my experience Prague is one of those places that people love to tell you that they've been to.

'Oh yes, *Prague*, *I've* been there,' they'll say, in an authoritative tone that they like to think makes them sound worldly – because going to Paris was '*so* 90s'. 'Oh yes, it's *lovely*. You should really go! It's so picturesque and beautiful!'

My introduction to Prague was a small park directly outside of the main station, Hlavni Nadrazi, which was full of scruffy-looking people spitting on the floor and urinating in nearby shrubbery. I suppose at least there was shrubbery. Thankfully the surroundings became a bit more pleasant as I entered the old town, where ornate towers reached up into the blue sky above, acting as route markers from the zig-zagging network of narrow streets below. It was off one such street that I found a dark alleyway with a large door that led along to an imposing stone staircase. At the top of this I found a pokey set of rooms that formed a hostel. A friendly man quickly checked me in and handed me a key and a well-worn floral towel. I carry my own travel towel, but when you're moving on so regularly it becomes inconvenient having to always pack up a damp towel, so this was a nice addition, despite the pattern not especially being to my taste.

Having dropped off my bag and newly acquired towel in a dorm room on the floor above, I set off back down the steps for some exploring, and to hunt down something to eat. It turned out that I was staying very close to the Old Town Square, which was busy with groups of sightseers taking in the picture-postcard surroundings. Staroměstské náměstí is undoubtedly a picturesque location, with its vast cobbled expanse allowing plenty of space for groups to gather for photographs or to sit around tables around the edges, taking in the variety of striking baroque and gothic architecture whilst sipping coffees or beers. I soon found myself standing next to a row of wooden huts on the far side of the square. One in particular caught my eye (or more accurately my nose) as it was offering freshly carved, spit-roasted ham. I was lured towards the slowly rotating animal as it gently sizzled above the coals; its skin crackling in the heat of the glowing charcoal beneath. (Apologies if you're vegetarian.) I briefly studied the menu (which was a little unnecessary as it really only offered one thing) and was quickly served. Whilst the succulent pinkish meat was undoubtedly the main attraction, I had expected some sort of accompaniment; a bit of salad to add some colour and textural variety, or perhaps a little bread. But no, this was a no-nonsense ham distributory: this was pure ham, delivered in an uncompromising style as a chunk of meat callously hacked off the charred beast and dumped inelegantly on a paper plate. To make matters worse I was then charged approximately four times what I had been expecting, clearly having missed the section of the menu that definitely didn't explain that the price shown was for a set weight; a weight that had been duly ignored and comfortably surpassed by the server. To cement the downturn in this now slightly distressing situation I was handed a plastic knife and fork. I cautiously took the plate over to a neighbouring table and began jabbing at the ham. The pathetically flimsy cutlery immediately snapped against the crisp skin of the meat. It was all rather reminiscent of my waffle incident in Brussels. I eventually had to resort to tearing apart the ham with my fingers like an animal. It was a far less dignified event than I would have liked, but as some consolation it did fill my hunger gap.

Having messed up lunch I set off to do some exploring. As I headed out of the main square I noticed that there was a gathering of people all staring behind me. I turned around to see a very large and ornate clock with lots of intricate dials set into the wall of a tower. I joined in the staring for a moment, before spotting some more people on a high up walkway at the top of the tower above the clock face. I concluded that this tower was climbable. I found a little entrance to one side where I was able to purchase a ticket, then slightly oddly I had to follow a little map on the back of the ticket to another entrance further along the street where the steps were located that led up to the top of the clock tower.

Prague's astronomical clock is the oldest working example of such a clock in the world, dating back to the early 15th Century. Leaning slightly dangerously over the top viewing walkway I could look down on the sea of eager faces that were watching for the hourly display of characters that appear from behind the face and strike the clock to signify the chiming of the hour. Unfortunately my birds-eye position and an inconveniently placed ledge blocked my view of the spectacle itself, but I was caught up in the second element of the event when I felt a tap on my shoulder. I turned around and quickly made space as a man in a decorative red outfit stepped up to the centre of the walkway and performed a brief trumpet ditty, much to the appreciation and applause of the crowds below. He then walked around to the other sides of the tower and did the same, each time getting more rapturous applause. He played for around 45 seconds in total. This has to be one of the most rewarding jobs I've ever encountered.

Edging past the crowds back on street level I headed away from the main square via a series of narrow streets that were lined with tiny shops selling the usual touristy gimmicks. I soon came to an ornate looking archway next to a tower, beyond which I saw evidence of a bridge. I'd heard that there was a famous bridge in Prague, and judging by all the flags and people lingering in its vicinity I suspected that this was it. The Charles Bridge is a stone bridge lined with imposing baroque statues stood on plinths along either side, beneath which are a number of archways that together span the Vltava River. Its significance stems from it being the only crossing of the river up until the mid 19th Century, and so it formed part of a key trade route across Europe. Although it has had numerous bouts of repair and reconstruction, the bridge has survived wars and floods, and now with more modern neighbouring bridges taking the motorised traffic, it is left free for visitors to amble across at their leisure.

As I crossed the bridge, admiring the variety of statues on the plinths and the rushing water as it broke between the arches below, I spotted another of the city's key attractions. It's hard to miss Prague Castle, because it's rather big. It also helps that it's up on a hill (which I guess you would expect for a castle). Apparently it's the largest castle in Europe, although it doesn't have a classic medieval form, but instead it consists of a number of palaces, churches and museums, all of which span a broad mix of architectural styles. I climbed up through the streets and the many, many steps and spent a while exploring the different courtyards that link up the various sections. Crowds were gathering to see inside the towering gothic Basilica of Saint Vitus and to explore the grounds that play host to countless other buildings that have formed the home of a variety of dignitaries over the centuries. There were a lot of queues I didn't fancy joining, and as the 'castle' didn't have enough turrets or crenelations for my liking, I decided to escape the crowds and head off into the neighbouring parkland. Poking up above the trees I could see what appeared to be a metal-framed watchtower. After the pristine grandness of the castle complex with its hoards of visitors and the popularity and resulting congestion of the Charles Bridge, the rickety-looking Petřín tower - the base of which is hidden away in the woodland - looked like a nice escape. More importantly though, you're allowed up the tower, and as I've already mentioned, I like being high. Built in the late 19th Century, the tower is said to resemble the Eiffel Tower in Paris, although it's only 64 metres high (240 metres shorter than its French counterpart), and there are less fountains and street artists surrounding this one. As I approached the base I saw a small girl drop her ice cream on the ground at the bottom of the steps, and then after bursting into tears she stood in it, which I suppose at a push did look vaguely artistic.

There were quite a few people milling about, but it didn't take long to ascend to the level that housed the lookout platform. This was just as well, as the narrow, semi-exposed creaking steps that wound dizzyingly upwards left little room for passing other people. Although not as glamorous a setting as the castle, the views were far better. I could see across to the palaces and basilicas within the castle walls on the other side of the hill, as well as the towers and rows of red roofs that mark out the old town. It was the vibrant tiling that drew my attention to the impending change in weather, as I watched the striking red colouring disappear in a line as clouds cast an ever-increasing shadow over the city.

Back out in the grounds of the tower I came across a small building at the end of one of the many pathways. To my surprise it housed a small funicular railway station that connects the top of the hill with the city at the bottom. I found a ticket machine, slipped in a couple of coins and took this neat, time-saving little ride downwards. Once at the bottom I made my way back towards the river, where a tram pulled up in front of me. At first I was irritated as I'd had every intention of crossing the road at the exact point where it had now stopped, but then I remembered that my funicular ticket entitled me to travel on all public transport within 90 minutes. I decided to make use of this, and so I quickly hopped aboard, just as the bell rang to signal the closing of the doors. I still find trams relatively novel, despite their increasing popularity across Europe. In London the Tube is the main form of transport, with buses serving as the above ground alternative, so getting to ride on a tram was helping to diversify my experiences of public transport. Unfortunately my instant decision to board the tram then quickly backfired. We turned left onto Most legií, a bridge that crosses the river via a narrow island, before promptly turning right again and setting off away from the Old Town. Realising this, I quickly rang the bell and jumped off at the next available stop. Whilst the tram ride had meant that I had got more use out of my ticket, at just under two minutes long I probably can't claim that this journey had substantially increased my knowledge of trams, other than now recognising the value in doing a little more research before blindly boarding every form of transport that shows up. As a final inconvenience I found myself slightly further away from where I wanted to be than before I had got on the tram.

Once back in more familiar surrounds I rustled up a relatively uninspiring meal at the hostel, and then I decided I would go out and paint the town red. I figured the best place for the painting to begin was the Old Town Square. It was a little after nine o'clock, which I had intentionally planned as to avoid the bar crawl that was due to begin at this time beneath the clock tower (according to the many people that had been trying to push leaflets about it into my hand earlier). I didn't want to spend my evening caught up in an enlarged stag party-style outing; I wanted a more innovative and *exciting* night out.

The square was almost deserted apart from a few Japanese tourists still milling about as they waited for the astronomical clock to chime. The outdoor seating areas were being packed away and the men and women who earlier had been eagerly trying to lure punters into their establishments with the promise of enticing refreshments had vanished. This wild and exciting night out I had sought amounted to me sitting alone in an almost-empty pub on the far side of the square from the clock, quietly sipping an over-priced beer whilst listening to the half-hearted slurs of what appeared to be a one-woman Alanis Morissette tribute act. Perhaps it was ironic, perhaps it was just bad luck. Sadly her heavily accented wailings failed to bring a spark to the characterless establishment, and instead the depressed air being grudgingly sucked in by the minimal yet overpoweringly miserable clientele discouraged me from sticking around for the encore. To complete a night that I had well and truly failed to paint anything closer to red than a pale magenta, the clouds that had been threatening finally released a sudden downpour to accompany me as I made my way back to the hostel. Thanks, Prague.

Thoroughly wet, I arrived back in my dorm room where I found an American girl sat in the middle of the floor. One of the things I like about travelling is the relatively meaningless conversations you can have in passing with people. You can chat away without paying too much attention to yourself or the other person, happy in the knowledge that it shouldn't dramatically affect your life as in all probability you'll never see them again. Sometimes you can be lucky enough to learn something interesting – a fact perhaps – that you can share as an anecdote around fancy dinner parties in later years, and this is of course a bonus. Unfortunately, meeting someone who after polite introductory acknowledgements begins a conversation by telling you that they have 'come to get away from things' isn't really what you want to hear. In fact I find this a pretty uncomfortable response to why someone is where they are. It could mean that they have a dark history, the explanation to which could be long and complex and may taint an otherwise pleasant (if rainy) summer's evening. It could mean that the person is a bit strange and believes that 'things' (whatever they may be) are out to get them, or it could mean that they are on the run, and that we should expect

Interpol to bang on the door at any second. It really is a conversation stopper. I bit my lip, made a semi-understanding 'hmmm' sound and stared awkwardly at the ceiling.

'Hey! You missed out earlier,' she blurted out, with the dark undertones of her earlier statement vanishing in an instant, 'I met these two dudes and we went and had tequila shots and discussed philosophy!'

It sounded like a god-send that I'd missed this. The idea of drinking tequila and talking philosophy was not an appealing one. She'd also used the word 'dudes'. Thank goodness I had opted to waste my evening sitting alone in a bar listening to the mis-representative ramblings of Alanis.

'Oh right! Sounds...yeah, shame.' I said, mustering all the fake-disappointment I could.

'There were some amazing clouds...' she added, having flicked unnervingly from dark and mysterious to 'spacey' via an explosion of enthusiasm. She struck me as a little emotionally imbalanced.

'Oh...wow. Yeah...clouds are...pretty cool.'

Clouds aren't cool. They block sunshine and rain on me. Although I am a bit partial to a well-formed cumulus.

'Hey, let's play cards!'

She had suddenly taken a decisive twist, but this was okay, because I like playing cards.

'Yeah, sure.'

'Cool! Have you played this before?'

Of *course* I'd played cards before. It's the staple form of entertainment for a backpacker. I never go on a trip without a pack of cards.

She then enthusiastically pulled out a set of cards from her bag, which on closer inspection had weird coloured shapes on them.

They didn't have any numbers on them, or hearts, or diamonds, or clubs...or even any spades! I had *never* seen cards like these before.

From how Jess described it (as I discovered was her name) you had to find 'sets' based upon the cards you were holding in your hand and those that were gradually revealed from the deck on the floor. Apparently you had to match some elements of the cards, but not all of them, because that was wrong. Sometimes it was colours, sometimes shapes, sometimes both, or sometimes neither. Sometimes you had to match the *number* of shapes. The 'game' took the form of me cautiously moving my hand towards a recently up-turned card on the floor, waiting for Jess' nod of approval or head-shake of despair, whilst she would frantically grab at cards and lay down 'sets' without any obvious rationale. I hadn't been this confused since trying to interpret the Brussels metro map, and needless to say I lost every game, without ever particularly understanding why.

I was soon released from Jess' clutches once I had firmly demonstrated my ineptitude for matching basic shapes and colours. I was still none the wiser as to why the Czech Republic was the obvious choice of 'getaway' destinations from Wisconsin, but I had concluded that she probably wasn't a major crime threat. As I got ready for bed I also decided that although it had been pleasant, I would leave Prague and press on with my journey of rail-based discovery the next day.

Chapter 15

Brno, Czech Republic

My next stop was mildly significant, as for once I wasn't crossing any borders to get there, and so it was also the first place I was visiting on this trip that wasn't a capital city. I had chosen Brno for two important reasons; firstly I was intrigued about how you pronounce it when I first noticed it on the departure board, as from what I could tell, despite only being four letters long, there really didn't seem to be enough vowels in it. The second reason was because I couldn't see any other trains that would conveniently take me in my preferred south-easterly direction.

I was once again confined to a compartment for the three-hour trip along the tracks to the Czech Republic's second city. Unfortunately the age of the train was reflected in the heavily distorted PA system, and so the muffled announcement that preceded our arrival gave little further indication of how the city's name is pronounced, but I decided to get off anyway.

It wasn't the smartest of stations, but I suppose this is what happens once you leave the big travel hubs. Outside I was immediately faced with the tricky task of crossing a very busy road. There were a lot of buses, and also my new-found nemesis: trams. After the mess-up in Prague I didn't want to chance jumping cluelessly onboard (despite their quaint appearance and alluring bell-ringing) and so instead I attempted the slightly daunting pedestrian crossing. Thankfully I survived the onslaught of public transport and made it safely to a wide shopping street, Masarykova, on the other side. I found myself walking past what I assumed was a fashionable clothing outlet, with windows filled with numerous manikins set in trendy stances. They were also wearing clothes (I probably would have questioned their grasp of basic marketing had they not have been), many of which featured baffling (but no doubt trendy) phrases on, such as 'LOL for you'. However, more significant than this was the price: this particular t-shirt was the equivalent of £2.50. I decided that Brno would now be my favoured location for future clothing purchases. I then re-read the slogan 'Lol for you', and decided that actually, it wouldn't.

Further along Masarykova I came to a large open paved area, that with my ever-growing knowledge of historic cities I took to be the main square. It had a number of architecturally striking buildings around the sides, and a statue on top of a tall pillar on a plinth towards the centre. Intriguingly, it also had a lot of sand, and also quite a lot of deck chairs. It is at this point that I should bestow some handy geographical insight upon you, and highlight that Brno is approximately 250 miles from the nearest coastline. In fact it's possibly one of the furthest cities from the sea in Europe. Perhaps it was therefore out of irony (or sympathy) that it was chosen to host what was, according to a skilfully carved block of sand, the *Festival Sand Golden*! It really was quite the spectacle. Behind an enclosure of railings stood a series of sand sculptures, each with a little information plaque that described what it was and who made it. It appeared that sand artists from across Europe (but predominantly Germany) had converged on the Czech Republic's second city to shape piles of sand into a variety of indeterminate shapes. They were impressive, but I didn't quite understand why they were here. More puzzling still was the small 'DJ hut', where a man in flowery shorts was dispensing drinks to himself (as well as some pretty terrible Euro dance music) in front of a collection of empty sun loungers and in the presence of what I took to be the local radio station. Strangest of all though, was that there weren't any people. I was more or less the only person taking any interest in this bizarre spectacle, and I can't say that I was fully caught up in the *Festival Sand Golden*. If only Jess had been here, because she would probably have found logic in the sandy shapes in front of me, or at least been able to quickly match them into pairs.

The absence of people seemed to be a recurring theme in Brno. I continued my explorations around the centre, but aside from a few window shoppers (all the shops seemed to be closed) and a few people strolling in a nearby park, the city was pretty much deserted. Even the cafes and restaurants that I infrequently passed on my wanders gave little indication that they had done any trade today. It was all a little strange. In many ways the city had some similarities to Prague, such as the architecture as an obvious example, but there was a far more laid-back feel to it. Actually 'laid-back' is perhaps a little misleading; *dead* would be more accurate. Even the outdoor bar and adjacent collection of benches that were lined up underneath a large beer-sponsored awning that sprung out from the side of a church wasn't drawing in any punters. Weird. Maybe I had just missed the big party that accompanies the arrival of the *Festival Sand Golden*, and now Brno was in a city-wide hangover. Maybe everyone was actually inside the clothes shop near the station, queuing to get their hands on the latest wacky-sloganed t-shirt. Perhaps everyone was on holiday, 'Lol-ing' at me for being over 250 miles from the nearest beach in the height of summer. Whatever the reason, I was a little disappointed in my first encounter of Brno.

I did find one attraction that briefly occupied me; a castle that was discretely sat on top of a leafy hill to the west of the main street. I wound up the pathway towards it, passing a few stray locals sprawled out beneath the trees as I went. I carried on through a stone archway that led to a pleasant viewing point next to an ice cream hut. As I should have expected, it wasn't exactly doing a roaring trade. In fact it probably risked being put out of business by the girl sitting on a nearby bench who had chosen to bring her own sandwich and bottle of water. I took in the view out across the city for a few minutes, made a half-hearted attempt to get inside the castle (to no avail), and then made my way back down to the station. From what I'd seen it wasn't just a vowel this city was short of. I didn't see much point in sticking around any longer.

Chapter 16

Vienna, Austria

I let the departure board decide my next destination, partly because I live on the edge, but also because it wasn't clear which city would be convenient to get to from Brno. High up on the wall of the station foyer was an old-style mechanical flip board. Every few minutes it would noisily scroll through its collection of numbers and letters as new destinations and times were selected. It was quite exciting watching these place names I didn't recognise (let alone could pronounce) slowly form above me. Eventually a name emerged from the rattling movements of the board that I did recognise and could pronounce, and it was one that appealed: Wien.

I'd been to Austria once before around 12 years ago, on a day trip where we had taken the train from Munich to Salzburg, over the border in Austria. I have two main memories from that that brief visit; sitting in the calming surrounds of a biergarten eating wurst, and the constant references by those around me to it being the location for the setting of *The Sound of Music*. Certainly one of these is a happier memory. Another vague association I made with Austria, and specifically Vienna, was sitting around chatting with my family one Christmas Day, whilst in the background my Nan was quietly watching a classical music concert, *Live from Schönbrunn*, on television. I assumed it was a pre-recorded programme judging by the sunshine that was casting shadows across the vast, neatly gravelled courtyard in front of an immaculate palace facia, as well as the smart, but equally summery attire of the musicians and audience. It certainly looked like an impressive place, and so between virtuosic music, grand palaces, appetising food and beer gardens I had high hopes that Vienna would be a good destination to visit, and so I set off on another train journey through some light central European drizzle.

Arriving in Vienna brought some relief, because which ever way you choose to spell it, 'Vienna' or 'Wien' both have a very balanced vowel-to-consonant ratio, and for that I was glad. Another bonus was that I was back in Euro-land, so I could switch back to the notes and coins I had left over from Berlin. My wallet was starting to bulge from the remnants of the six different currencies I had used so far, and my brain was finding the constant demand to convert prices between them all a little hard to keep up with. There was something else that was in contrast to Brno, too; there were people everywhere, all bustling past each other as they went about their days. Men and women in suits rushed about with briefcases, families were fighting to control children as cyclists weaved around them, and there were even a few backpacker-ish looking people like myself. In a bid to escape a group of slow-walkers in front, I turned down a narrow alleyway that cut in between two shops and came out beside St Stephen's Cathedral, towering up out of the shadows that shrouded the little archway I'd just emerged from. Around the front of the cathedral it became clear that I was in the centre of the city, as I was stood at a confluence of wide pedestrianised streets that sprouted off in different directions from Stephensplatz. Signs and fascias for hotels, restaurants and shops littered the sides of neighbouring buildings, with outdoor seating areas full of lunchtime diners below them.

As I looped the square I suddenly became aware of an unusual soundtrack cutting through the din of the crowds. There was a strange blend of operatic wailing and heavily distorted hip-hop beats. I turned to my left and noticed a large gathering of people in a circle, where through a brief gap I spotted a sound system and a group of guys jumping about with microphones whilst draped in masses of gold jewellery. I then turned around to face the opposite street and noticed a neatly presented elder-lady in a dress, who was forcefully delivering an acapella soprano melody whilst stood next to a shop doorway. She was able to compete with the amplified MC-ing of the hip hop collective thanks to a subtly attached mic pack that was clipped to the waistband of her dress, the other end of which was plugged into a small speaker on the pavement next to her. This was busking like I had never seen (or heard) before. I flicked between looking at each of the two performance camps, each with their own loyal (if temporary) listenership. There were no shabbily dressed people strumming a battered acoustic guitar in a lacklustre manner; no warbling of the vaguely distinguishable sounds of *Oasis' Wonderwall* or a song by *Travis* – this was high-class busking: carefully considered outfits, clean, crisp choreography, professional sound equipment and a high level of tone and performance. If I had any pre-conception about Vienna, it was living up to them gloriously.

It took me quite a while to make my way along the lively Kärntner Straße, where I passed a further two operatic singers, a percussion group and a string quartet. The street entertainment was of such a high standard that I decided to stop off and eat an authentic Viennese wiener schnitzel as I drifted between the eclectic musical offerings. If there had been hills in the vicinity, they certainly would have been alive with the sound of...erm, instruments.

Having satisfied two of the elements I associated with Vienna – music and food – I pressed on to tackle the third: the palace. I figured it was quite large, and therefore it couldn't be too hard to find. I quickly came across a striking, light stone building at the end of Kärntner Straße. It was impressive with its many arch-topped windows and decorative fountains, but there wasn't any space for an orchestra as it was right next to the main road. As I turned the corner to face the front of the building it became apparent that this was Vienna's Opera House. I carried on, following the traffic-filled Opernring as I had spied some intriguing domes poking up above the other buildings a bit further along. After following the kink in the road that marks the border around Innere Stadt, I found myself surrounded by several potential candidates for a palace. Every direction I looked in there was grand baroque architecture, with more archways, columns and domed roofs than anyone could ever hope to fit in a single photograph. I turned left and walked between two of the more prominent buildings, both facing on to a central garden with a large plinth in the centre. I took it in turns to wander over to each building to inspect what they were. One was the Natural History Museum and the other was the History of Arts Museum. I'm sure both of these contained fascinating exhibitions, but I was determined to find the palace, and so I crossed back over the main road and walked through a set of arches, which led me through to a building that I immediately became convinced must be what I was looking for. Its huge facia had an inward curve, which is surely the ultimate indication of residential opulence. But there was a problem: there was no expansive forecourt where you could set up a large-scale musical performance. For a start there were too many horse statues that would get in the way, and it also appeared to be tarmaced over and currently in use as a car park. I couldn't see this being how a palace forecourt moonlighted. The building also looked too grey in colour, as I remembered a more yellowish tint to the building I saw on television. This was not the palace. I trudged back through the archway, catching a sign that revealed that this was yet another museum, and that the area I was in was the museum quarter. This was a very apt name. Vienna certainly has a lot of museums.

I was starting to get impatient with my apparent lack of palace-finding intuition, and I was about to re-consider my plan when I caught sight of a road sign. It had a large arrow pointing off towards the south-west of the city centre, and above it was the word *Schönbrunn*. Finally I was in business.

Despite my initial enthusiasm at finding the name on a sign, it turned out to be a bit of a trek from the city to get to the grounds. I mainly stuck to the main road for navigational purposes so that I could follow the road signs, which meant it wasn't the most relaxing or prettiest of routes, but after an hour of urban-hiking and traffic-dodging I finally came to a large wall with neatly trimmed grass in front of it. On the other side of the road was a train station called *Schönbrunn*, which would have no doubt been the stop for a train that would have whisked me out here from the city centre in a matter of minutes, but never mind. I came to a large open gate, and upon stepping through this grand entrance I found myself on the edge of a massive courtyard brimming with people, and there was an immaculate yellow-beige palace centred across the far end. This was *definitely* it.

Schönbrunn Schloß was built in the 17th Century and was a summer residence for Empress Sisi, the former Queen of Hungary and Empress of Austria. The baroque residence is now Vienna's most popular tourist attraction, with the 1,441-room palace and expansive grounds drawing in over two and half million visitors a year. I also discovered that the grounds host live music concerts in the summer, which was reassuring to hear. It certainly had the space for it. I strolled over to the front of the palace, transfixed by the sheer number of windows it had. I then realised that the crowds to my left were actually forming a massive queue leading up to a side entrance. There was no way I would be getting inside to see the many rooms behind the windows today. Thankfully there are also massive gardens that are free for visitors to wander through. I made my way around to the back of the Palace, making a brief stop to go up a raised balcony at the back of the building from where I could take in the vastness and near-perfect symmetry of the gardens. It extended up past a series of beautifully manicured flowerbeds to a raised stone promontory, beyond which the striking arch-filled presence of the 'Gloriette' sat centrally at the top of the hill. I made my way up to it, dodging past the numerous horses and carriages that were elegantly carrying the more discerning visitors around the grounds. I trudged up the hill on foot, the pathways zigzagging along to soften the gradient and allow more time for taking in the many impressively maintained sections of the grounds. From up on the stone plinth that the Gloriette sits on (inside of which there is a café with prices equally set for the more discerning visitor) there are further picturesque views down to the palace, and from this high up position on the hill it's neatly framed by the city beyond. The sun then made a very convenient appearance from behind the clouds, highlighting the light-coloured brick work so that the palace and vibrant horticultural surrounds lit up in a very striking manner. A break in the symmetry then caught my eye to the left-hand side. It appeared to be a dense array of hedges with a disproportionate number of people milling around them. I headed down to investigate.

It soon became apparent that parts of the garden have been cultivated for more than just visual effect. This particular section had been set aside to entertain, with the centre-piece being a maze, carefully cut out of the dense shrubbery. I bought a ticket from the little entrance hut and made my way to the start. The centre was just a stones-throw away, clearly indicated by a raised wooden tree house-type platform. This looked easy. I set off confidently along the pathways. As I strode purposefully down the narrow isles between the neatly trimmed hedges young children darted about, shouting and squealing in mild states of hysteria. They didn't have a clue what they were doing – they were *amateurs*. Not me though, because I was a *grown-up*. *I* had successfully navigated my way across Western, Northern and Central Europe. I even had previous maze experience, having successfully completed the Hampton Court Palace maze in the late 90s. I was a pro, and these children could learn much from my wiseness.

Five minutes later and I was further away from the centre than when I had started, which in itself was concerning given that I had started at the edge, but mainly it was irritating. I then looked up to see the children that I had encountered running cluelessly about at the start, now happily peering out from the central platform. The crafty little bastards. This was very annoying. A few more wrong turns and dead ends later and I eventually made it to the finishing point. I climbed the steps to the central platform as the shrill voices of the children grew ominously closer; my enthusiasm for the maze decreasing further as I surveyed the scene from the high up vantage point and realised just what a small area it actually occupied. I stood for a couple of minutes assessing where I had come from (and where I had gone wrong), before the irritating screams of the children drove me to abandon the tree-top hang out and to descend back down into the acoustically-dampening surrounds of the maze's thick hedges. To try and make amends for my poor effort I decided not to take the easy route out, and instead I tried re-tracing my steps to find the entrance the hard way. This didn't go to plan either, and if anything it took longer than it had on the way in. I had firmly lost my maze stripes.

Beyond the maze I found a labyrinth, where a series of low hedges wound around a relatively small rectangle, and yet somehow it took the best part of 10 minutes to reach the centre. Other features included a collection of pathways with various puzzles and challenges etched into the ground. It was all quite entertaining, and an unexpected twist to the otherwise very formal surrounds of the palace. I could understand why it was such a popular attraction, and I hadn't even witnessed a live concert, or even been *inside* the palace for that matter.

It was getting on for six by the time I made it back to the centre of Vienna. The street musicians were still out in force, although they now appeared to be dressed in evening gowns, with song selections seemingly chosen to suit the change in mood that this time of day brings. I walked beyond Stephensplatz, past further ornate buildings and cobbled streets until I found myself next to a river. It was here that I saw something that caught my attention. I hadn't planned where to stay that night and so I was open to ideas. Seeing the mini-catamaran moored to the edge of the river as it bobbed gently up and down helped to steer me. It was offering a quick service along the Danube to Bratislava, which is a mere 40-odd miles downstream. I realise that again I was sort of breaking the rules by taking a boat on a trip that was about train travel, but I reasoned that taking the train on this leg would have been an inefficient use of my rail pass as it was only a short journey. I also thought that it would be a good opportunity to experience Europe's second longest river, and one that connects a number of the countries that I planned on visiting during this trip. So with my conscience almost clear, and with a one-way ticket soon booked, I utilised the free wi-fi to sort out accommodation in the Slovakian capital. There only seemed to be one option available, which was the intriguingly named *Hostel*

Spirit. It certainly sounded very positive, and so I awaited my next journey with much excitement and anticipation.

Chapter 17

Bratislava, Slovakia

It should have been a glorious arrival in Slovakia. I should have been thrust dramatically into the heart of the city by the boat. I should have been adorned in god-sent sun rays as I disembarked onto a smart promenade surrounded by local dignitaries and well-wishers. Well okay, I probably shouldn't have expected this, and I'm not one to want a fuss, but a bit of sunshine wouldn't have gone amiss.

My trip along the Danube had been speedy, but low, dark, rain-spitting clouds had increasingly blocked the intermittent patches of blue sky as the latter stages of evening drew in. The river water had an uninviting brown murkiness to it, and the lush greenery that had been flourishing on the river banks during the earlier part of the boat ride now looked slightly gaunt and haggard. It was therefore a rather drab arrival as I clambered off the boat and found myself in a grubby back street surrounded by broken paving stones and rather inartistic graffiti. A jaded looking sign that half-heartedly proclaimed the destination hung wearily above the docking platform. I tentatively trod along a heavily pot-holed road next to some shabbily dressed people who were lingering around a worn, paint-chipped railing beside the river. A raindrop dripped into my eye. All in all it was pretty tempting just to hop back on to the boat and return to Vienna. Glorious Vienna, where every building resembles a palace and the street buskers wear robes and sing operatic medleys.

But I was sure Bratislava would prove this introduction was a mere teaser, and soon its true magnificence would reveal itself. I ambled along the street, taking myself away from the river and into the historic Old Town where I came across a group of Japanese tourists. They were gathered around a statue of a man coming out of a drain. Things weren't getting any better. The Japanese tourists found this fantastic however, and each insisted that they were photographed standing next to it (at least twice) with their hand resting on the statue's head. I stood there bewildered. I then turned around and saw a fast-food shop with 'I Tomato Pizza' written on the sign. My bewilderment increased. A couple of turns later and I arrived in a very quaint square, which featured a nice fountain as its centrepiece and a surprising number of flags that weren't that of Slovakia. There was a French flag, a Greek flag and a Japanese flag (much to the excitement of the drain-obsessed tourists behind me), and on one side of the square was a building that was occupied by the *Vienna Insurance Company*. I had a quick look at the map that had come with my boat ticket to make sure I was actually in Slovakia, because they didn't exactly seem to be bragging about it. This square also had another excellent statue, this time of a man whose hat had fallen over his eyes as he leant drunkenly against a bench. It was safe to say that I was not understanding Bratislava.

I carried on along a pleasant cobbled alleyway that was lined with bars and restaurants, and then I went through a neat little turreted gateway. It was while passing one of the bars that I overheard a British voice from inside, loudly declaring that he'd 'had sixteen pisses already today'. This was impressive. I had only had two. I was proud of him. I was proud to be British. I then remembered that Bratislava was one of these destinations that budget airlines have picked up on, and as a result it has become a haven for stag parties. Vienna really did seem more than 40 miles away.

I quickly made my way out of the tourist epicentre and headed further north in the direction of where I understood my accommodation to be. I crossed over onto a main road where I found myself outside a relatively low-key palace. In front of it was a large metal globe that seemed to have large chunks bitten out of it, as well as a ceremonial pigeon perched on top. I stopped to scratch my head, and then I carried on. I was briefly halted again whilst I was negotiating a number of tramlines that cris-crossed over at this slightly complex intersection when a large spark flew off the connector rod of a passing electric bus. I sighed. It was getting darker, and the weather less favourable. I appeared to be entering an area that was evidently popular with vandals as the level of graffiti increased and the buildings looked more dishevelled and in need of some serious renovation. I also noted that all of the road signs were giving directions to places that were *not in Slovakia*. I'm not sure if this was telling, but I was apparently following the route to Vienna in Austria, and Brno in the Czech Republic – precisely back the way I had come. I was then distracted by a statue of a skeletal figure holding a giant pair of sheers. It was all a little creepy.

I turned off along a side road and passed a neglected playground next to a building surrounded by barbed wire and broken glass. It definitely looked like I had chosen to stay in an excellent part of the city. I made a mental note to congratulate myself once (or if) I made it to the hostel. A swift walk under an ominous looking bridge that was home to a large amount of rubbish and general eeriness and I emerged on the other side to a quite frankly shocking sight. Through the rain and miserable grey surrounds that I had just come through, I suddenly found myself stood in front of the most bizarre concoction of architectural design (if you could call it that) that I had ever seen.

Describing it as topsy-turvy wouldn't be doing it justice. A complete miss-match of random brightly coloured shapes and materials had been slung together in a mass of anarchic construction, and hanging off one of its many edges was a sign. *This* was my hostel for the night. *This* was *Hostel Spirit*.

I got it. To make up for the grimness of the area they had tried to counter it in the extreme. But it was terrifying. The name 'Hostel Spirit' somehow made it so much more horrific, too. Regardless, I had booked a bed, so there was nothing for it but to try and find a door in the mass of steel, stone, polystyrene, papier-mâché...and whatever else they had cobbled together to 'construct' it. Inside I was greeted by a lady who didn't speak English, and so to get around this she used *Google Translate* to determine what I was doing there. To be honest I was starting to question that as well. She then charged me (contrary to my booking) for the most expensive hostel room I had ever stayed in, before asking me to fill out a form consisting of basic admin questions. At the bottom of the form it requested the 'signature of alien'. I paused, and then did a quick squiggle that I hoped would represent what an alien would do if it was given a pen for the first time. The lady seemed happy enough with this, and so I made my way up to my room, which appeared to have been decorated by a three-year-old girl. Paint splotches were trying to masquerade as 'art' and the hopscotch carpet went no further in justifying the price tag. I slumped on to the bed, my head resting against the rainbow-covered wall as I found myself wondering what it would be like to have been to the toilet 16 times during one day. I reckoned that if the man in the bar shared his impressive feat with the local council they might be tempted to make a statue in recognition of it.

After a short rest I decided that it was time I went in search of something to eat. Slovakia conveniently uses the Euro, and so I fished about in my backpack to dig out some relevant currency. I made the stupid mistake of tipping up my bag, spilling coins out across the heavily patterned hopscotch carpet. After patting around the various coloured squares and lines to reclaim my money, I had a quick wash and then headed out of the door. As I reached the end of the corridor I heard rustling in one of the rooms to the right. Peering through the open door I found a guy battling to deploy a bed sheet. Upon hearing my footsteps he swung around and immediately dropped the sheet.

'Hi, I'm Mark! Do you wanna go for dinner?!'

I should have been suspicious from the start. Exchanging names is something you don't often do when moving around a lot (let alone at the start of the conversation) because it just doesn't have much significance when you meet so many people for such a short time. I also found it slightly odd that he had immediately invited me to dinner before I had even spoken. I was wary, but ultimately I did need something to eat. I tentatively agreed.

Mark was an(other) American. He wasn't trying to get away from anything though; he was just having a short break from studying in Prague. He had short spiky hair and a gangly frame that bobbed along in a rather bizarre manner as we set off back to the Old Town. Mark had with him a scrap of paper that had on it a scribbled map of how to get to an eatery someone back in Prague had recommended. This was the type of useful insight you look for from strangers, and so combined with my ever-improving scribbled-map-reading skills we made a useful team as we successfully located the character-full surrounds of the *Slovak Pub* along Obchodná, just north of the Old Town. It may not have had the most innovative name, but the dimly lit network of wooden-beamed rooms and corridors were packed with youthful urbanites, most tucking in to what looked like an exciting array of dishes. We managed to find space at the end of one of the long bench seats in the corner of a room on the second floor. Mark then declared his second piece of useful knowledge.

'We should have Halušky! It's the local dish!'

'Yeah, okay, sounds good.' I replied. I had no idea what this was. It could have been fried giraffe testicles for all I knew, but I like eating local food, and having studied the expansive menu with its barrage of unusually accented words I was none the wiser as to what was on offer, so at least this gave some clear direction.

Mark placed our order, and then I quickly added in a request for a beer, as I felt I needed something to detract from the occasion, having suddenly become very aware that I had agreed to come out to dinner with a random guy who had just ordered my food for me. Mark immediately said that sounded nice and he'd have one too. The soft background music and candle on the table between us wasn't helping the slightly awkward atmosphere, either.

Thankfully the food arrived quickly and proved to be delicious. Halušky is a dish of potato dumplings, and ours were topped with bacon bits with some mild seasoning. We speedily ate up the slightly chewy dumplings with the crisp bacon, washing it all down with some equally tasty Slovak beer. We paid up, which itself was a strangely enjoyable experience once I had worked out that the large plate of food and two rounds of beers had cost around a tenth of what the minimalist meatball dish had cost in Stockholm. Bratislava was rapidly going up in my estimations.

With a head full of strong dark ale, we dropped down into the Old Town in search of further traditional Slovakian experiences. We found these in *Casa Del Havana*; the local Slovak-Cuban salsa bar. Inside we found a group of rowdy thirty-something Brits, carelessly pouring tequila shots down their excessively tight sleeveless vests as they jumped about to self-conducted football chants. In an attempt to drown out their tuneless wailing, someone behind the bar flicked a switch to introduce some minimalist techno beats, which beautifully complimented the authentic Latin American feel. We stayed just long enough to down a pint of warm, watery beer before quickly escaping out of the door.

It was becoming very apparent just how much Bratislava was equipping itself for the drinking-visitor market. The quiet narrow streets that I had walked through on my arrival were now dotted with chalkboards filled with drink offers. Neon signs flashed above pokey doorways and scantily clad women wearing too much make-up ushered passer-bys into their designated establishments. It was a bit like being back on a budget flight, which of course is fitting as it is the emergence of budget airlines that has brought this business to cities like Bratislava. Mark and I tentatively followed some crooked stone steps down into a basement bar, where we lined up another couple of drinks before taking shelter in one of the cave-like booths to one side. This place seemed quieter than the Cuban bar, but no sooner had we sat down then a band of middle-aged men appeared on a small raised platform on the other side of the room. After some shuffling about and plugging in of instruments, they eventually broke in to a rather uncoordinated rendition of *ABBA's Waterloo*. The night was now deteriorating rapidly. I edged along the cold stone bench and into the darkened corner, gripping my pint glass ever tighter. Mark on the other hand was nodding his head enthusiastically, mesmerised by the distorted Slovak-Swedish melodies that were emanating from the cheap PA system on the wall. Just as the band were building towards a muddled finale, the sound suddenly cut out, along with all the lights in the underground bar. It appeared to be a power cut, or as I would describe it – a godsend. After a few minutes of glorious silence, the lights and sound made an uncomfortable return. I decided to call it a night, leaving Mark to carry on his journey of poorly re-hashed Euro-pop enlightenment, whilst I headed off back to the child's art-accident that housed my bed for the night. I thought that I would probably need a good night's sleep to have any hope of being able to face more of Bratislava.

I woke up early, wide-eyed and feeling slightly jittery. Perhaps spending a night in the brightly-coloured surrounds of *Hostel Spirit* had an effect on me, but it meant I was up, packed and ready to go in super-quick time. I bid farewell to the misshapen mess that had accommodated me at such unnecessary expense and set off back down to the city centre. Aside from a smashed pane of glass from a bus shelter window, the Old Town had returned to a quaint, unassuming scene after its night of debauchery. The weather was decidedly less gloomy than it had been the previous day, and there was a marked difference in the overall feel to the place. The roads looked tidier and the pavements less cracked, the buildings smarter and more attractive with their brightly painted exteriors. Even the graffiti had a more artistic quality than it seemed to have on my arrival. I walked back past the Grassalkovich Palace, pausing outside. It had looked a little crest-fallen in yesterday's failing light, but this morning it had more of a vibrancy to it, as the nation's flag gently flapped about in the breeze above the gate. It's amazing how a night of cheap Eastern European beer, bad Swedish pop music and trip-inducing dorm room walls can affect your perspective on things. I later discovered that not to be outdone by Vienna's palatial prevalence, the crisp, railing-fronted baroque home of the Slovakian president also has a significant history of hosting famous composers, including Joseph Haydn, whose string quartet nicknamed 'The Joke' I studied at school. It's a piece that still sometimes gets stuck in my head thanks to its cheerful melody, distinctive Rondo form and 'light-hearted' false ending.

I continued to walk around the west side of the Old Town, where I came across St Martin's Cathedral, from which the faint sound of choral song was emanating. I crept through the large wooden door mid-service, and stood quietly at the back to benefit from the cooling surrounds of the cavernous building after my heated exertions in the ever-strengthening sun. A sermon followed the singing, which was delivered from an ornate parapet far down on the left hand side, but in all honestly it went a little over my head. Another hymn followed, and I took the opportunity to delve into my pockets to pull out any loose coins I had left. Later today I planned to leave Slovakia and Euro-land, so this felt like a worthy way to relieve myself of what soon would be unnecessary currency. However, as I grabbed a handful and withdrew it from my jeans, I caught my wrist on my belt strap. I thankfully avoided an outburst of blasphemy, as not for the first time in this city I spilt a lot of coins. Whilst the floor in the cathedral was not awkwardly decorated as to mask their whereabouts, it *was* made of solid, highly polished wood. This moment of carelessness also beautifully coincided with the end of the hymn, and so the abrupt silence was sharply broken by the sound of noisily scattering coins. *A lot* of people turned around to stare at me. I in turn bowed my head symbolically. I'm not sure if I had lost faith, but I had *certainly* lost face. I collected up the coins, slipped them into the collection box and headed back out of the door.

If there was one thing I didn't expect to see as I walked along in the shadows beneath Bratislava Castle that sat perched on the rocky hill above, it was a UFO. This is what I saw, however, hovering just beyond the roofs of the Old Town. I followed what remains of the city wall down towards the river, edging along a busy intersection as

I struggled to find an easy route. Instead of reaching the bank of the Danube however, I found myself in a grubby bus station underneath a raised section of road. I crossed over the worn tarmac and cut between the battered posts and shelters that formed the various deserted stopping areas, before finding a set of steps that led upwards. I eventually came out onto a concrete walkway. Out to the left I could see the flowing water of the Danube, indicating I was now on a bridge. I walked along it, admiring the view out to the river and less so the graffiti along the concrete block work that surrounded me on the other three sides. As I reached the other side and descended the steps I peered up through a gap in the concrete and found that the UFO was in fact balancing on a large metal frame rising up above me. At the bottom of the steps I found a little glass door. Upon pushing my way through it I was greeted by a very smartly dressed lady with a clipboard.

'Are you eating or just seeing the view?' she asked politely, and in a manner that suggested she had been expecting me.

'Erm, just the view, please.'

I instinctively handed over a couple of Euros and was given a ticket in return. I was then ushered into a small lift, where she pressed a button and then left me to it. I was caught a little off guard at having come across such a well-turned-out person lurking under a grotty stairwell, but seconds later there was a soft beeping and then the doors of the lift opened. I stepped out and climbed a few steps until I reached a doorway that led out on to a small rectangular platform. It was very blustery, which was probably understandable given that I was now 85 metres up, overlooking the *Most Slovenského národného povstania – the Bridge of the Slovak National Uprising*. It is also known as 'New Bridge', which is a little easier to say (and write), although the bridge is now over 40 years old. From what I could work out I was now directly above the main capsule of the spacecraft, which I deduced was where the restaurant was to be found. Aside from its slightly unorthodox appearance, my favourite thing that I learnt about the bridge and its imaginatively placed restaurant and viewing area, is that it is officially the shortest member of the *Federation of Great Towers*. A fine claim to fame indeed.

Aside from the bridge-tower, there was very little indication that the south side of the Danube offered any real attractions. From the top of the tower I had enjoyed the views of the Old Town to the north, with the castle gleaming in the sun and the various baroque towers and facades scattered amongst the hidden cobbled streets below, but the south had only offered views out over rows of communist tower blocks. Now back at ground level though, I discovered an expansive park running beside the river. The trees quickly blocked out any views of the bridge and the ominous concentration of tower blocks further to the south, and I could hear birds chirping away from within their branches and the rustling of leaves as a light breeze subtly made its presence felt. It was incredibly tranquil. I thought I'd already encountered a few different sides to this city, but this was yet another unexpected offering from one of Europe's newest capital cities.

At the far end of the park I found the deteriorating remains of a stadium. I clambered over the broken gates, through the mangled turnstiles and found myself on the heavily overgrown grass of the pitch. Despite being sunny and the middle of the day there was still an unsettling feel to it. I climbed up some concrete steps that led up through one of the decrepit stands, being careful to avoid the broken glass from beer bottles, and sat for a few minutes on one of the few remaining intact seats. In less than an hour I had gone from a ridiculously brash hostel to an ornate cathedral, on to a lovely expansive park via the world's shortest tall tower, and finally on to an abandoned sporting venue. The historical complexity and bizarre characteristics of this city had won me over. Despite Vienna undoubtedly being a culturally magnificent destination, there was a strange amalgamation of developing identities and overarching oddness about Bratislava that I liked. It was a city in the process of stamping its mark on Europe. It is a city that has incurred dominance from Austrians, Germans, Hungarians and Czechs through its turbulent history, but it was now gaining prominence in its own right as an independent capital, although it now faced a new invasion: that of the British, mass drunken male collective. Good luck.

Chapter 18

Budapest, Hungary

I was a little irritated to discover that Bratislava's main railway station was back north of the city centre, practically adjacent to *Hostel Spirit*. To avoid trudging back up the main road again I chose to branch off through some residential streets, drawn up a hill on the western side by the sight of a statue. It seemed like an easy point to get to, but as with my *Schönbrunn* maze experience, things aren't always as straightforward as they first appear. It took me a breathless half hour of cutting through suburban estates, woodland paths and a frustrating amount of backtracking before I finally made it to the top of the hill, where I found *Slavín* – a memorial to the Soviet soldiers who died during the Second World War. This statue of a soldier stood on top of a huge plinth is a far more impressive and sizeable monument than the view of it from down below in the city would suggest. The determination you need to find it also makes arriving at its base, as well as the views out across the city from the top of the hill that much more rewarding. I wandered about through the neat gardens and walkways beneath the monument for a few minutes, savouring the views and the calm, deserted surrounds of the hill top before making my way back down through the steep hillside streets towards the station.

There was no head scratching over my next destination; I wanted to follow the flow of the Danube and head down-stream (or down-track) to Budapest. A short wait and I was soon once again in the slightly socially awkward surroundings of a train carriage compartment. This one was busier than the others I'd been in, and I spent the first couple of minutes trying to find space for my legs, as it was a little cramped. In the end I managed to configure them so they alternated between the other passengers' on the opposing row, which may sound like I have more legs than you would consider normal, but ultimately everyone seemed happy with the arrangement.

The late night and early start was starting to take its toll on me as we rattled along through the Hungarian countryside. The seats had little side cushions on the headrests that were very inviting to my weary head, and so I leant into one and let my eyes close. When they opened again I was a little shocked to find the man sat opposite me (who had been wearing a shirt and tie as he studied some documents he'd pulled out of a smart black brief case) was now wearing bright red flowery shorts. I can't have drifted off for more than 10 minutes, and I certainly hadn't been aware of any movement. I assumed, or rather *hoped* that this slightly odd transition hadn't taken place right in front of me in the compartment. There surely wasn't the legroom.

Budapest was sunny and so all was well. Admittedly I was being half-heartedly pursued and lightly berated in a foreign tongue by a scruffy fellow who had selected a rather pungent alcohol-scented mouthwash, but I'm sure he meant well. The train had arrived on time at the main station in Pest on the east side of the Danube, and I was preoccupied with tracking down my accommodation. The streets were busy with people, and my focus on the task in hand meant I was yet to catch sight of the city's naming counterpart, Buda, situated on the western side of the river. Budapest is another Eastern European destination that has become increasingly popular in recent years, with people drawn by its rich historical and geological features, and of course assisted by the budget airlines.

You might even say it's 'the Prague for people who have already been to Prague having already been to Paris several times', but you probably won't say that, and that's okay too.

I enthusiastically counted off the roads along Erzsébet körút as I matched them to the Hungarian edition of my scribbled-map anthology. I then began passing roads that by all accounts I shouldn't have been, so I stopped, turned around, and eventually found a pair of large brown doors set back from the pavement, next to which was a small sign with *Big Fish Hostel* scrawled in colourful, wacky lettering on it. These rugged, ominously barred doors did not reflect the chirpiness of the sign, but the name was right, so I pressed the buzzer and was soon making my way up a wide staircase and being enthusiastically ushered through a first-floor doorway. It was a very chirpy lady who greeted me – not like the doors, but a lot like the sign - and her cheery nature continued as she showed me to my dorm room and then on to the four bathrooms that were available to me. I appeared to be the only resident, but I certainly wouldn't be short of washing facilities, and this was undoubtedly a great relief. I made a mental note to recommend the plentiful toilet supply to Bratislava's drinking fraternity, if ever I should have the pleasure of running into them again. Tour complete, I returned to reception to collect my key, where I noticed a sign on a blackboard next to the front door that read 'Carnival Tonight!' in more exciting lettering.

'What's the carnival?' I enquired, nodding towards the sign and thus asserting my fantastic awareness to all those present.

The lady (who was the only person other than myself in the hostel, and so I assumed was the author of the sign) peered cautiously at the words, her eyes narrowing behind the thick-lenses of her glasses.

'I…I don't know... I think…it is…carnival!'

She either had an excellent grasp of sarcasm or mild amnesia. She continued, still sounding puzzled by her own handy work. 'You wear...costume...and drink?' she said, nodding at my apparent lack of costume, before shrugging, and then returning to her little reception desk where she started smiling inanely at all the bookings she clearly didn't have on her notepad. It sounded like it would be a real blast.

I set off into the pleasantly warm surrounds of central Pest, and after wandering down to the banks of the Danube I sat down on a bench to have a look at the map the receptionist had handed to me during the bathroom tour. After a couple of minutes a man in a long dark jacket and a low-rimmed black hat sat beside me, and started muttering to me in hushed undertones. No one likes an undertone – hushed or otherwise – especially not in summer. I turned to face him and smiled blankly. His stern expression made me stop smiling, however.

'Tourist?' he grunted.

I was, but somehow I didn't appreciate the way he implied it with such venom. Perhaps it was the hushedness of it, or maybe the undertones, but I started edging along the bench away from him. I then suddenly became inexplicably fascinated by the church I had just noticed behind me. Sensing the occasion could develop into one in which I may soon feel a sharp point in my side and hear a menacingly whispered instruction to 'keep walking' in my ear, I did the classic 'pretend to take a photograph' move. In an awkward twist though, as I pointed the lens at the church (the wonderfully pronounceable Belvárosi plébániatemplom) I realised that in fact it was actually quite a nice church, so I proceeded to back up the fake photograph with a real one. Sometimes basic tourism instincts can override the best-laid decoy plans. I then put my camera away and hurried over towards Erzsébet híd, which is one of several bridges that span the Danube to link Buda and Pest. I whizzed around the stone wall at the base of the bridge and jogged up the steps, pausing to glance back over the wall and down to the promenade below. The man had risen from the bench and was now converging with his hands in his pockets on another shifty looking man in similarly suspicious attire. Everyone else was in shorts and flip-flops, and so they really stood out in their unseasonable trench coats and rimmed hats. The men headed towards the bridge and then swiftly changed direction multiple times. It probably looked like a human game of 'Pac Man' - if I'd played computer games in the 80s and had any real grasp of what that game actually involved. Regardless, I didn't want to stick around to find out what they were up to as I feared it would ultimately involve my wallet or medical insurance, so I quickly headed up on to the bridge and started making my way out across the river. This wasn't as easy as I had hoped as the strong winds made my getaway less than slick. I blundered along, swaying from side to side as I balanced trying to take in the very picturesque scene along the river whilst trying to evade my would-be pursuers. After a frantic few minutes of backward glances, forward advances and photographic chances, I made it across to the other side and the hillier terrain of Buda. Here I was immediately greeted by an unsavoury looking man with straggly hair. He shoved a cardboard cup in my face and from his creased mouth gurgled 'Money!' Suddenly that two-person carnival back at the multi-bathroomed hostel didn't sound like such a bad option.

Buda and Pest have differences that go beyond their opposing positions on either side of the river. While Pest exhibits all the hallmarks of a busy city going about its day-to-day business with its cafes, restaurants and shops lining the busy streets, Buda has a far more relaxed air to it. It seemed a lot calmer since I'd crossed the river and begun ascending the steep hill on the other side, although this may have been largely down to me being confident that the Budapest pests were no longer targeting me. At the top of the hill was the Freedom Statue - another nod of remembrance to Soviet occupation - standing proudly in front of the Citadella as it keeps watch over the city. As nice a spot as it was, I'd actually gone up the wrong hill. Confusingly this fortification does not sit on top of Castle Hill where I had been aiming for. There are two main hills in Buda that rise up adjacent to the Danube, and it quickly became apparent from up next to the Citadella that it was the other one I wanted. I dropped back down to river level via a stretch of parkland and then found a back road up towards my intended destination.

It was late evening as I completed my second ascent, and the sun was slowly setting behind the hills of Buda and casting an attractive red glow across Pest. I stood in front of the Hungarian National Gallery, set in grounds of the impressive (if once again not overly 'castley') castle, admiring the striking gothic façade of the Parliament building that was sat prominently on the bank of the Danube further up stream in Pest, its red roof and light coloured bricks being vividly lit by the fading sun and reflected in the water.

I spent some time meandering around the network of quaint cobbled streets on top of Castle Hill as I looked for the entrance to the attraction that had lured me up there. A friend had told me about a labyrinth of tunnels that run under the hill and this had intrigued me. I'd seen my fair share of castles on this trip, but aside from my initial train journey from London to Brussels, the trip had been largely absent of tunnels. I hoped this would change here in Hungary, but I was struggling to find any indication of how you might get to them. A couple of signs pointed broadly off in various directions, but ultimately my search proved fruitless, and a shadow had by now firmly cut across Pest as the hills shielded the last of the suns light. I was starting to get tired from all the ups and downs of

Buda, and so I began heading back down the hill. It was along this road behind Castle Hill that I suddenly noticed a small, unassuming wooden door in the hillside. There was no sign, and it looked like it might be a service hatch of some kind, but I crossed over the road to have a look anyway. Expecting it to be locked, I yanked hard on the handle, but to my surprise the door creaked open, the sound echoing along what appeared to be a dark stone passage. Beyond the first few metres there was little to see, but I could just make out a faint orange glow. I had no idea how close it was, but I decided to investigate. I stepped inside and slowly edged along the dark passage, the door closing behind me with a bang, which instantly cut out all the natural light as I began feeling my way along the rough stone walls. It was noticeably colder in here, and there was a strong smell of damp. The glowing proved to be much further than I had anticipated, but as I finally got close to where I thought it was, I heard a very loud, shrill scream. The silhouette of a woman then appeared against the wall, outlined faintly in the orange light that now evidently marked an abrupt bend in the passage. The source of the ear-piercing sound then sheepishly emerged from behind the wall, before quickly hurrying off in the direction I had just come from. I continued around the corner and into the darkness. More orange glows appeared, which on closer inspection revealed themselves to be lanterns attached to the walls. A few turns later and I arrived at a small glass fronted booth. A sign then confirmed that I had found the entrance to the tunnels, albeit via what may well have been the emergency exit. I peered through the glass and was immediately confronted by the unwelcoming glare of an angry looking man's face.

'Closed!' he grunted.

And that concluded my visit to the Budapest tunnels.

Back at the hostel the 'carnival' was in full swing. A straggly paper streamer hung from a door and a small green balloon rolled about by a table leg. There was also a small boy sitting on a chair sucking on a crayon whilst shaking an empty beaker. I think Rio would be disappointed in the *Big Fish Hostel*. Still, my decision not to invest heavily in an extravagant costume looked like a wise one. From the quiet foyer I heard voices coming from the lounge. I walked in to find a small group of people gathered around a table drinking out of plastic cups through colourful straws. One of the girls turned around as I entered.

'Hey! Come join us! We're about to have Pálinka!'

'Giraffe's testicles?'

'What?'

'Never mind. Sounds great!'

I joined the group at the table where we were all given a shot glass with a colourful liquid inside. We counted to three - in Spanish, for reasons that weren't immediately clear - and then knocked back what we learnt was a traditional Hungarian spirit. It was strong and fruity. I hope this wasn't what the child in the other room had been drinking from his beaker. The group consisted of the hostel co-owner (who was looking after the crayon-eating child and whose partner in business was currently away setting up a hostel in Spain, which possibly explained the Spanish connection) and a group of American girls who were on teaching placements. The girls then hurried off to get ready for a night out, so I went over to the sofas in the corner where I got chatting to a Spaniard.

Giorgio was in his mid-thirties and had been a banker in Madrid. He'd grown bored of his work though, and decided a month ago to quit his well-paid job in the Spanish capital and hit the rails of Europe. He didn't have much of a route in mind, but he was loosely heading towards Istanbul. So far he had passed through Spain,

France and Italy among others, taking in any cities that took his fancy along the way. I very much enjoyed listening to Giorgio's tales. Here was someone who hadn't done a lot of travelling before, but had decided that there was more to life than being stuck in an office all day, regardless of how financially lucrative it could be, and so he had abandoned it all for a backpack and a book of European train timetables. We sat around exchanging stories from being on the rails and he usefully informed me that the paid sections of the tunnels in Budapest were in fact pretty disappointing, and so I had done well to avoid them.

After around half an hour a group of girls came bounding into the room in their pyjamas. I was a little confused as I wrongly mistook them to be the girls who had gone to get ready to go out. As it turned out this was *another* group of American girls who were on teaching placements and were also staying in the hostel. I was now convinced that I was travelling through the *United States of Europe*. Contrary to the other group though, these girls had opted for a night in, and quickly nestled into the gaps in the sofa between Giorgio and myself. The carnival was turning out to be quite the pleasant event, until one of the girls selected a film for us all to watch, which meant we were then subjected to two hours of *Bridget Jones* and her sodding diary.

There was no sign of the streamer or the balloon the following morning: carnival season was clearly over. As some consolation though, a new sign had appeared on the back of the door and it caught my eye. This one took the form of a poster that was proclaiming a 'great discount' on one of the local thermal spas. Aside from bridges, hills and tunnels, Budapest is home to many geothermal springs. After the ups and downs of my Buda exploration yesterday, and then of course having to sit through the stressful ups and downs of Bridget's crazy life, a warm soak in a naturally heated spa sounded like the perfect tonic. The lady on reception kindly sold me a heavily discounted ticket and I set off into Pest.

I took a looping route to the bathhouse, because I wanted to go back down to the bank of the Danube to see the parliament building close up. I walked along past the Opera House and across to the riverbank, taking a detour across the distinctive Chain Bridge. This impressive suspension bridge was the first to cross the Danube and it gained its significance as a landmark of the city through its engineering feat, but also due to its physical and symbolic linking of East and West Europe. On the other side of the bridge the road disappears underneath Castle Hill into a large tunnel, and beside this I noticed a funicular railway heading up to the top. A much-celebrated bridge, a grand castle quarter on top of a hill reached via a funicular railway; I was certainly getting a sense of déjà vu. I could see why people who liked Prague would be drawn here.

Back on the east bank I walked north along the river, unexpectedly passing a poignant memorial to Jewish suffering in the Second World War. A collection of cast iron shoes are scattered along the promenade, which I later found out represent a harrowing event where Jews were lined up on the river's edge, asked to remove their shoes and then shot, causing them to fall into the Danube and be carried away in the current. Not for the first time I found myself learning unexpected histories about a place through casual wanderings, all of which were helping to fill in a few more pieces in the complex (and often unnerving) jigsaw of Europe and its intricate past.

Despite being the tallest building in Budapest, as well as arguably the most striking and (at least politically) important, I was surprised at how quiet it was around the parliament building. I didn't see anyone else other than a couple of security guards, who were meandering around the steps whilst looking thoroughly disinterested in their posting.

After the surprise of the shoe memorial and the chilly breeze whipping off the river around the eerie quietness of the parliament building, I felt it was time I got a move on and went to find these thermal baths. I checked the map and set off, zig-zagging haphazardly through the streets. I could have taken a bus or the underground metro line, but I was once again enjoying my urban wanders through the interesting surroundings of the Hungarian capital. I found my way on to the busy Andrássy Way, heading in a north-easterly direction towards the City Park, passing the subtly named 'Museum of Terror' along the way. The entrance to the park was grandly marked with the sizeable statues and columns of Hero's Square. On either side of this vast open space are two art galleries. After establishing certain similarities of Prague, I now sensed a touch of Vienna. I'm probably not the first person in history to make an Austrian-Hungarian link, though.

Beyond the galleries and columns the city park opened up, with pathways cutting between the trees and patches of grass filled with families enjoying the fine weather. I quickly found the Széchenyi thermal bath, recognising its distinctive neo-baroque design from the poster I'd seen at the hostel. It was built in the early 20th Century, and the interior looked like it had been altered little since then. Ornate mosaics hung above the smartly tiled flooring that guided me over to a formal wooden desk, where I was promptly told to go away. Perhaps they wanted me to marvel at its exterior just a little bit more. The second entrance I tried seemed remarkably similar to the first, but at least this time I was allowed to purchase a discounted ticket with my voucher and proceed down the steps to the changing area. Luckily I had packed my swimming shorts for this trip, and although a little dishevelled from being repeatedly stuffed into my backpack, my travel towel was just about acceptable for this rather grand bathing experience.

Stepping out of the conservatory-style doors I found myself in a large inner courtyard, with the yellow walls of the indoor bath houses and changing rooms bordering the outdoor pools on all sides. I put my towel down next to a sun lounger and climbed down into the main pool. The heat of the water hit me sharply. The baths (the largest of their kind in Europe) take their water from two naturally occurring springs that were at this precise moment heated to over 70 degrees Celsius, according to the thermometer on the wall. Gradually I lowered myself deeper into the water and waded out into the centre of the pool before dunking myself fully under. Once I'd adapted to the temperature I looked around to see what other people were doing. There was a wide ledge running around the edge of the pool that allowed people to lie down with just their heads showing above the surface, enabling the water's apparent medicinal qualities to get to work on their bodies. This was obviously the most desirable position to have, and was therefore fiercely competitive. I watched as other bath-goers scouted out the areas where space was either likely to become available, or where they felt they could feasibly squeeze in to. Elsewhere in the pool I observed groups of locals were gently bobbing about as they caught up on the week's goings-on. A group of elderly men were huddled in one corner of the bath, engrossed in a mid-afternoon chess game, whilst some were content to simply lie about in the sun around the edge of the pool, ignoring the allure of the warm water altogether.

I spent about 20 minutes in the pool, my arms cutting through the water as I occasionally dared to break into a swim. This was short-lived though, as there was not the space to embark on any especially athletic strokes, and I had also suddenly become fearful that I was breaking spa pool etiquette. It was pointless hoping I'd manage to get an edge-spot, and so after watching the minute hand on the large white clock face opposite me slowly edge towards the hour mark, I decided that I'd spent enough time wallowing about and so I got out of the pool and went to get changed.

Refreshed and potentially medically improved, I continued my clockwise loop of the city, eventually arriving at Budapest Keleti Railway Terminal. This seemed like a good opportunity to book a ticket for the next leg of my trip, and so I went up the steps and through the doors that led through to the grand station atrium. I followed the platform along past a number of small refreshment shops until I found a door beneath a sign that said 'ticket office'. I walked over to it and pulled it open, where my freshly renewed, spa-induced sense of relaxation vanished in an instant.

Chapter 19

Budapest to Belgrade

It wasn't a pretty sight as I stepped inside. It was a large room, but every inch of floor was covered with backpacker. People and bags were strewn everywhere, becoming indistinguishable from one another as a mass of jaded faces and fabrics. I thought the ticket office at Amsterdam Centraal had been busy, but this demonstrated a whole new chaotic level to train travel booking. I managed to carefully step between a couple of bags and legs to rip off a ticket to assign my place in the queue (if that's what you could call this). I checked the number and then the screens above the counters. Perhaps not surprisingly I was in for a long wait, and judging by the sweaty and anxious faces of those around me, there may be bigger problems in store, too.

I'd so far largely taken for granted how easy it had been to arrange my train travel across Europe. Once I'd got hold of my InterRail pass I had done very little planning, and more or less just made up my route up as I went along. Beyond Amsterdam there had never been an issue of not finding a suitable train or seat availability, and the process of choosing a destination, getting on board a train and then filling in the details on my pass had all become part of the hassle-free routine I had become accustomed to. But I was now getting to the business end of my trip, and although I'd been doing my best to squeeze in as much as I could in this limited window of space I had between jobs, there now really was more than ever little scope for error, as I was due to start work in only a few days time. I reckoned that missing my first day because I was stuck in Hungary would not be getting off on the right foot.

I managed to find a small patch of wall next to a timetable board that I could lean against. It looked like there were four ticket windows in operation, each home to a weary looking station employee that seemed to be doing a lot more head-shaking and sympathetic shoulder-shrugs than I found encouraging. It was very hot and stuffy in the airless ticket office, which was adding to the level of discomfort that everyone inside was clearly experiencing. The numbers above the desks edged up painfully slowly as I occasionally transferred my weight between each foot at regular intervals as my legs began to ache. I had to be careful though, because as soon as anyone moved slightly, a new clump of bag strapping or a limb of a traveller would quickly fill the gap. Things were pretty desperate. Groups around me took it in turns to man the post whilst others went off in search of refreshments. I couldn't risk leaving in case I missed my precious slot at one of the windows and I was getting increasingly uneasy about the prospect of not being able to go where I wanted, when I wanted. I just had to stick it out and hope for the best.

Budapest is clearly a hub for travel across the continent. I overheard several long-distance destinations mentioned, including Berlin, Warsaw and Bucharest. I didn't hear any mention of Zagreb though, which is where I wanted to get to. On one hand this was concerning as I began to wonder if it was even a destination served by trains from Budapest, but on the other hand it was promising, as perhaps it was an option, but just a less popular route so I would be able to get a ticket. I drummed my fingers against my leg and stared dumbly at the digits on the number-display, willing them on. In one way I was glad I didn't have my bag with me as there was such little space, but it would have been nice to have my mp3 player or a book as a distraction to occupy myself with as I waited. Instead all I could do was watch the agonisingly slow-to-change ticket number screen on the wall, or observe those around me. A group of Germans were up at the window closest to me, desperation growing in their voices as they were informed that all the trains to Munich were booked up. An irate Australian lady was talking loudly on a mobile phone, clearly taking out her frustrating on whoever was on the other end of the line.

'This is bloody ridiculous...no...what?...no they said there's no space...well I don't know what the hell I'm going to do!'

It wasn't encouraging.

A French girl next to me was muttering to herself, and beyond her a mute couple were frantically signing to each other. My knowledge of sign language is limited to a few letters and phrases, but I'm sure some of the actions they were doing were post-watershed.

An hour and a half later and a greasy film had taken up residence on my forehead. The soles of my feet felt raw through my flimsy shoes and my throat was painfully dry. At last the display was approaching my number. Part of me was getting excited about it nearly being my turn, but I was also becoming increasingly nervous, as the fate of my plans would soon be revealed. My number flashed up. It was time. I hurried over to the window.

'Hi, could I book a ticket to Zagreb for tomorrow, please?' I said, my eyes squinting in a pointless attempt at shielding myself from impending bad news.

The man tapped away at his ancient computer, before blowing out his cheeks and shaking his head in the same manner that I'd witnessed so many times since being in the ticket office.

Shit.

'No, we have no more spaces' he said.

'Shit' I muttered.

And that was that. No other options. He looked dead behind the eyes, no doubt numbed from emotion after having to deliver similar news to so many people before me. The dull look of painful realisation that I returned must be one that gets you down after seeing it from so many people throughout the day.

So I had a problem. I couldn't get to where I wanted to go, and not only that but I had waited *an hour and a half* to be told it. I couldn't face the prospect of having wasted all that time to be rejected in less than 15 seconds. I frantically looked around the room in grim desperation. I then caught sight of a piece of paper through the glass of the ticket window. It had 'Belgrade' scrawled on it, followed by '22.20'.

'Is there a night train to Belgrade?' I asked, pointing at the piece of paper.

The man seemed surprised by my continued presence. His eyebrows went up and he nodded.

'Which day does it run?'

'There is one tonight and there is space' he replied, cleverly anticipating my next question.

Without thinking I semi-shouted, 'I'll take it!' as if fearful that if I left it more than a few seconds he would retract the offer or it would suddenly sell out.

He casually tapped at his computer a bit more and then wrote me out a ticket. This was brilliant, and *much* more exciting than getting a train in the morning to Zagreb, because now I was taking a *night* train! So what if going to Serbia meant heading in completely the wrong direction to where I needed to be going; I had once again battled with adversity and I would come out better off. Assuming that I did *eventually* make it back to London in the next few days, anyway. I was better off, because now I would once again have the thrill of catching a night train through Europe, which was something that I hadn't done for many years.

For many people a holiday begins once you arrive at your destination. You can finally relax once you've dragged your bulging suitcase up that last flight of stairs and collapsed on to your hotel bed. Or maybe even *that's* too soon, and it's only once you're draped across a sunlounger on the beach or next to the swimming pool with a cocktail. For me though, when I was growing up, holidays started at three o'clock in the morning when I had to get up, grab my bag containing various bits and pieces to entertain me for the journey (and maybe the odd piece of clothing) and bundle into the car to set off to wherever it was we were going. I would then excitedly draw away throughout the car journey as Dire Straits played on the cassette player until staring at the page made me feel a little sick and I'd have to stop and look out of the window. It was all part of the fun.

The point is that I find the journey a massively important and enjoyable part of going away; whether that's marvelling at the cleverly designed meal trays on an aeroplane or running about on the deck of a ferry getting covered in sea-spray – it was the sense of anticipation of what lay ahead; it was all adding to the adventure; it was all great fun. This hasn't changed as I've gotten older, either. Many people claim to enjoy travelling, but really they just like *being* somewhere, or preferably somewhere else. For me though, so much of it is about the journey, and this trip certainly focused on journeys; with all their ups and downs, unpredictability and unusual encounters along the way - and no train journey offers all of these things like a *night* train journey does!

One of my favourite holidays was when I was 12 years old, and my family and some friends of ours went to Italy. We stayed in a great resort on the outskirts of Florence, where we spent two weeks splashing about in the pool, visiting lots of cathedrals and eating a lot of pizza and pasta. But what really made it stand out for me was how we got there. We drove to Folkestone, drove onto a train that went under the sea, drove on to another train and then travelled overnight to Italy. It was *brilliant*. Not only had I been in a car that was on a train that had gone under the sea, but then, as I kicked a football around with my friends in front of the station in Calais, I watched as our car was driven on to the top deck of a double-decker car-carrying train carriage, before we jumped into the passenger section and set off across France and on to Italy. This was *surely* the future of holiday travel.

As it happened, it wasn't. The service soon went bust and car-carrying night trains are now practically non-existent. Admittedly they did have their flaws. Our train was significantly delayed and even ran out of food, so we had to get by for most of the 16-hour journey on French raisin biscuits. We also found out that they had blocked up the air vents, which meant it got pretty hot and stuffy onboard. This was apparently because it wasn't unknown for thieves to fill the train with gas to knock passengers unconscious during random night stops, so that they could come on board and rob everyone. Upon arrival in Italy one family found that their car's windscreen had been broken. Apparently it wasn't uncommon for kids in Paris to throw stones at passing trains from bridges at night.

Looking back it was a rather dodgy and inefficient way of travelling, but I remember more about that train journey – the tiny cabins with their three-high bunks on each side that folded down to make seats; playing cards in the foodless-buffet car; the random stops in the middle of nowhere; staying up late and running up and down the narrow corridors and flushing the toilet in the end carriage and watching its contents shoot out over the first vehicle that had the unfortunate position on the front car-carrying carriage (sorry!) – than I do about any plane I've flown on, hotel I've stayed at or beach I've dug a hole in. It was uncomfortable, unreliable, dangerous and it took bloody ages – and I'd loved every second of it.

I was therefore very excited about my impending journey back on a night train. I hurried back to my hostel to collect up my stuff, and to jump on a computer to book a hostel for the following night in Belgrade. The lady on reception even kindly refunded my now un-necessary second night booking at the *Big Fish Hostel*. I thanked her, and wished her well for the next carnival. I arrived back at the station early, ready to stock up on a few reserves for the journey. I wasn't going to have the luxury of a narrow fold-out bunk to sleep on, because I was doing this backpacker-style and travelling 'seat only'. I picked up some bottles of water and a few snacks and then headed out to the distant and eerily dark and deserted platform 11. I walked past a cleaner who was shuffling along, despondently picking up litter beside the train as it sat idle in the station. The lighting barely reached out to this seemingly forgotten platform, and there wasn't much more coming from the train either. I hoisted myself up into a carriage and began manoeuvring along the narrow corridor that ran down one side of it. It was another compartment set-up, and so I peered through the windows to find a suitable cabin to hole myself up in for the night. It was pointless really, because they were all the same, and more significantly, all empty. I chose one, slid open the door and slumped down next to the window. In the gloom I could see the dated seat fabric was well worn, and decorated with what I presumed were cigarette burns. The walls were discoloured and scuffed and the window heavily smeared. I toyed with the idea of switching on the light to deter anyone from joining me. Normally I'd welcome company, but as this was a night train I wanted the space to stretch out. In the end I left the light off as I decided that I didn't want to become too aware of my dirty surroundings.

I sat in darkness as the seconds ticked by, and then at 10.18 – just two minutes before our scheduled departure time – an elderly lady noisily slid open the door to the compartment. *My* compartment. She was short but quite portly, with rigidly combed back grey hair. I would have put her in her late 70s, her heavily wrinkled face screwed up as she muttered away in Hungarian. She was not alone either, as she had with her the quintessential OAP trolley bag, which quickly took up residence on top of my left foot. The lady continued to mutter angrily to herself as she sat opposite me, seemingly oblivious to my presence even after she had rudely switched on the harsh yellow-white bulb above the door. I sensed I had a long night ahead. My misery was further compounded when, soon after we creaked unnervingly out of the station, another pair of Hungarians entered the compartment, stealing more precious potential sleeping space. They sat beside me and began flicking through some sort of brochure. The light flickered on and off as we jolted from side to side. I wasn't convinced we were even travelling on railway tracks such was the ferocity of the vibrations and sideways motions.

Twenty minutes passed in uncomfortable not-quite-silence. The two late-comers then suddenly got up and left the compartment, leaving me alone with the crazy lady. The extra space was encouraging, but I didn't feel altogether safe being left alone in this confined space with her, even now her mutterings had been dropped in favour of frantic grape eating. She aggressively tore the grapes off their stems from a brown paper bag next to her as she stared fixated at the floor. She looked mildly possessed. I turned to face the grimy blankness that was the window and the night beyond.

As the journey wore on I quietly stretched my legs out as far as I could along the now empty seats beside me, and curled up with my face against the seat back. I was doing my best to shield my ears from the old lady, as no sooner had she devoured the last grape then she'd flopped over to one side and begun loudly snoring. Perhaps she had mistakenly bought rohypno-grapes.

At around two in the morning I was interrupted from my intermittent slumber by another bout of unceremonious jolting. The train had come to a standstill, but it felt like it was now being shunted repeatedly. I twisted my aching body around so I could peer through the window. The darkness combined with the scratches and marks on the glass made it difficult to see anything, but I could just about make out the rough outline of a person lingering near the train. I instinctively pushed my bag firmly up against the vent under the seats. I then heard the distinctive low-pitch rumble of a diesel engine getting closer, before the shadowy form of a train engine rumbled past on a neighbouring set of tracks. I fumbled about on the seats for my thick jumper and pulled it over my head, suddenly aware at how cold the compartment had become. There were further rumbles and shunts as we were pushed forwards and backwards for around 10 minutes. I lay back down and squeezed my eyes shut.

Suddenly my head jerked against the back of the seat. The coarse grain of the harsh commercial fabric rubbed painfully against my nose and cheek. The cold, bitter air sent shivers through my extremities as I slowly tried to adjust to the dark surroundings. I had no idea what time it was, but the juddering had stopped. The reverberations through my torso and the low grumbling of the engine had stopped. Everything had stopped. Everything, except a sharp, slapping sensation against my right leg. As I gradually regained consciousness I started to turn. Well, as much as I could. Pain surged through my left hand side. I was sprawled out across the seats, my hands trapped somewhere behind me, my legs semi-coiled to retain any warmth my weary body could muster. Through the darkness the anguished Hungarian wailing grew in volume until it dominated my thoughts with ear-piercing clarity. That was until the heavy footsteps cut them short. There was a flicker of movement in my peripheral vision. My neck was bent awkwardly as I strained to come to terms with what was happening. Suddenly there was silence. The wailing had stopped abruptly. The door was then forcefully thrust aside to reveal a silhouette, faintly outlined by a dim, tungsten glow. The looming shape of a heavily built figure filled the doorway. The only sound now was heavy breathing: *my* heavy breathing. The figure turned slowly towards me, the faint light source from behind briefly catching on something metallic to its lower right side. The barrel of a gun.

I was now very alert. The figure in the doorway stood there expectantly. I looked over and saw the old lady was holding something in her hand towards him. I suddenly realised what it was: a passport. Evidently this had also been the implement used in the leg-slapping. It was now apparent that she had been very kindly alerting me to the fact that we were at a checkpoint, and this man was part of the slightly creepy security patrol. The man hit the switch on the light as I faffed about in my bag to retrieve my passport. Squinting under the depressing glow of the compartment light I felt its familiar form, buried deep inside my bag. I managed to slide it out and hand it over. He flicked through the pages and then paused when he got to the picture. He took a couple of glances at me and then back at my passport, sniffed, and then thrust it back into my hand and left the compartment. I made the bold assumption that we had now arrived in Serbia.

Chapter 20

Belgrade, Serbia

It would be fair to say that my night train adventure had successfully lived up to the hype. It had the drama, the discomfort and the unpredictability of my previous night train experiences, and perhaps most importantly it also had that real sense that I'd travelled a significant distance (which of course I had) to reach yet another contrasting country in Europe. The lack of sleep and grubbiness of the train had left me far from refreshed as I emerged into the hot, humid surroundings of the Balkans, but this only made it feel more like I had earned my arrival in a new and exciting place.

While Prague and Budapest may be the current destinations of choice for many UK city-break seekers, Belgrade is yet to make a significant mark on the tourist radar. This was reflected by the contrasting emptiness of the station's ticket hall, where I swiftly picked up an onward ticket to Zagreb for the following day. Back on a workable schedule, I was now free to enjoy my bonus stopover in the former Yugoslav capital. Another reason for the emptiness could well have been because it was six in the morning. Despite this early hour, the heat already had an oppressive quality to it, and combined with my tiredness it was with some strain that I dragged myself up and down the main street outside the station in search of a cash machine. The pavements were cracked and dusty, and I could feel all the uneven edges through the thin soles of my shoes. I became further aware of my feet when a short man in a worn beige jacket started sweeping them. I thought this was a little strange, but as I looked around I noticed that actually a very high proportion of the people I could see were sweeping. They were either very dust-conscious in Belgrade, or this was a new craze that has yet to hit Western Europe. I dubiously thanked the man, although he had actually made my shoes dustier than they had been before. He quickly moved on to sweeping a leaf further along the pavement, so I assumed I was free to continue.

Further down the road I found an ATM beside a newsagent style shop that was yet to open, and I successfully managed to withdraw some Dinar. Having not originally planned on visiting Serbia I wasn't sure what the exchange rate was, and so the amounts listed on the small screen meant nothing to me. I pressed one of the options at random, and then stuffed the high denomination notes that were duly dispensed into my wallet, and headed back past the station and into a small park. There were a few homeless-looking people sprawled out across the benches beneath the trees, but looking at my current state I was in no real position to judge. Beyond the park I found a small café linked to the neighbouring bus station. Thankfully it was open, and so I pushed through the door and bought myself an orange, taking a seat in the corner of the smokey room until it was brought over, as flies circled the tables around me. A succession of torn and drearily patterned curtains blocked out much of the early morning light from inside the pokey room, and so I quickly finished my drink and retreated back to the more pleasant surrounds of the park, where I sat on a stone bench and pulled out my book as I waiting for what I thought would be an acceptable time to try and check-in to my accommodation.

Conveniently my hostel was in a building opposite. Inconveniently it was on the sixth floor. Once I'd made it up all the stairs I was rewarded by a nice welcome into a friendly looking hostel. I was allowed to check in (which was a relief given how early it still was) and then I was immediately told that I could help myself to free Turkish tea and laundry. As nice an offer as this was, I was actually far more interested in trying out the shower after my long night on the train.

I got cleaned up and then bravely resisted the overwhelming temptation to crash out on the bed. I didn't want my body clock to get out of synch, and then noticing that the skylight directly above my assigned bed was rather worryingly being held open by a pair of scissors was also a contributing factor in convincing me not to lie down.

It had been pretty warm throughout my journey across the continent so far, but here in the most southerly point of my trip it had stepped up to a new level of heat and humidity, and it was still only mid morning. I traipsed along, picking roads at random to turn along as the high temperature mercilessly inflicting itself on me, quickly undoing all the good work of the shower. I stopped to buy a drink from a kiosk on the pavement, an incident that made a man grumble at me as I massively overestimated the price of a bottle of water, handing over what turned out to be an embarrassingly high value note for an item that cost the equivalent of 15 pence. I downed the liquid and felt it immediately evaporate back out of me as I found my way through to a pedestrianised shopping street, and followed it along until it finished abruptly in front of another park.

Kalemegdan Park is a maze of pathways that meander off in all directions. I picked one at random and let it lead me through the trees until I reached a striking viewpoint. I was next to a wall, on the other side of which was a steep drop and then a river that curved around below. It looked like I had made my way to the far end of what was now very clearly an expansive promontory, where the River Sava had its confluence with the Danube. As you may expect for a place with such a strong geographical position, there was also a fortress, and it was the upper ramparts that I now found myself edging along as I embraced the cooling breeze and looked out over the intriguingly named Great War Island, which far from looking especially war-torn, was in fact covered in very peaceful looking trees.

Further along the fortifications I came across a little tower. There was no obvious sign indicating what it was, but a small wooden door that was ajar was enough to tempt me over. I pulled it open and climbed the creaky staircase that occupied the narrow, dark space beyond. I slowly ascended the stairs that were dimly lit by a couple of rather decrepit looking bulbs that were loosely attached to the walls. As I neared a hatch of daylight at the top, the sound of gruff mumblings interrupted me. They got louder and increasingly angry in tone, so I stopped to look back down the stairs. A couple of flights below I saw the outline of a man shuffle out from behind what had been a closed door. He looked up and gestured at me, rubbing his fingers together. Ah, he wanted money. I guiltily returned down to his floor and followed him into the room. It was a very cosy little space, with dusty books and papers scattered across a desk and complex-looking charts and shelves of yet more books lining the walls. The small window to the hot summery scenes outside was dirty to the point that an aged lamp on the desk was needed to provide any light. This felt like the quintessential professors' study.

My lightly poetic in-head observations were quickly interrupted as the elderly man (who now revealed himself to have a pronounced hunch and a gloriously explosive white beard) jabbed at a small piece of paper on the wall. It had some Cyrillic script, and then a number. I handed him a coin and he stopped mumbling and clambered over some files to get back behind his desk. I now appeared to be free to carry on with my trip up what I now took to be an observatory, having parted with 21 pence. At the top I found a couple of little telescopes, through which I could see enlarged views of the trees on Great War Island, a man in a hat walking along a road, and the strangely empty lanes of an outdoor swimming pool that was down by the river. It wasn't particularly different from the views you got a few metres below on the fortress wall, but I decided not to kick up too much of a fuss given the very reasonable entry fee.

Leaving the fort I made my back towards the centre of the city. The sun was getting more intense as morning slipped into afternoon, and my already well-worn clothes were rapidly deteriorating further as they frayed and stuck uncomfortably to my body in the heat. I broke off from the main pedestrianised street and took shelter in the cool, air-conditioned basement of a fashion outlet. I negotiated my way around the outlandishly coloured shirts that hung on rails scattered around the floor, and then decided that I would mark the most southerly and easterly point of my trip by splashing out on a new outfit. A few minutes later and I emerged back out into the bright sunshine having bought a plain green cotton t-shirt for the grand sum of £1.50. That's right, it was *plain* – you can LOL for me all you like, but I didn't think I was cool enough to brand myself with a hip slogan just yet.

Back at the hostel and I was really starting to flag. The lack of sleep I'd had in the past two days was taking its toll, but again instead of giving in to tiredness I nobly accepted the hostel owner's kind offer of a free 'welcome' beer, and perched on one of the sofas as I chatted to her in between flicking through a 'What's On Belgrade' leaflet I found on a shelf next to me. I felt a bit guilty knowing that I'd just purchased a new t-shirt, as it seemed a bit of a middle finger to the free laundry service that she had been so clear in offering. I'm sure the stuffy room and inevitably high night time temperatures (twinned with a highly possible scissor accident) would ensure that my bed sheets would need a good wash in the morning though, so I took some solace in this.

Over the following hour the free 'welcome' beer turned into several 'firmly routed' beers. Unfortunately I had missed happy hour, so I had to fork out nearly 60 pence for each additional beverage. I was starting to get the distinct impression that Belgrade was a thoroughly well-priced destination. Aside from extra drinks I was also joined by a collection of other hostelites, although oddly enough, none of them were American. A couple of guitars then emerged and soon we were having a sort of mini festival, the likes of which would probably over-excite the good people of the *Big Fish Hostel.*

The hours slipped by as we strummed, sipped and chatted away until we were interrupted by a tall man who was wearing sunglasses on his head, despite it now being dark outside.

'Right, lets go' he announced, clapping his hands together as he stood in that decisive manner that immediately rules out any chance of refusal.

The rest of us looked at each other a little bemused, but we knew that you don't argue with someone who wears sunglasses when it's dark, because they *always* know the best things to do.

As it happened, he didn't, as 20 minutes later and we were all gathered around a bench in a very dark park, passing around a large plastic bottle of warm beer. According to the sun-glassed one, this was where all the trendy people in Belgrade go on a night out. In my experience it's where you go when you're 15 and have been kicked out of a house party, but what do I know? After all, I only wear sunglasses when it's sunny.

Many gulps of beer later, and our 'host' – who for the record I think would be the perfect consumer for the 'LOL for you' t-shirt range – decided it was time. Time for what, we didn't know, but at exactly a few minutes past 11.15 pm, we were off again, leaving the other trendy Serbs (and quite a few homeless people) to carry on their night of park bench drinking.

We were led like a group of rowdy children on a school trip down towards the river. For all we knew, having been plied with cheap Serbian lager we were about to be directed onto an abandoned boat and robbed before being pushed overboard. This would be terrible, especially as I'd chosen to wear my brand new £1.50 t-shirt. Still, the night was very hot and sticky, so a quick dip in the river didn't sound so bad. As it turned out we didn't get to the water's edge, but instead we found ourselves filing along a bridge above it. I then became aware of other groups of people heading in the same direction as us, and this built rapidly as we hit land on the other side, until we were part of a huge crowd, purposefully heading onwards - to what, we still didn't know. And then, suddenly, we did. There was a banner hanging over the road up ahead. The edges of the sign were concealed by the branches of the trees that it hung from, but as the route straightened out it became visible: 'BEERFEST!' it read. Ah, *Beerfest*. When I had been casually browsing the 'What's On' guide back at the hostel I'd seen the name mentioned. It stood out because it had promised an eclectic mix of music, including something called *Turbofolk*, which sounded very intriguing. I'd read that it was a huge festival spread out over several days in the expansive and pleasantly named 'Park of Friendship'. Yes, Belgrade has a lot of parks.

The man in sunglasses stopped to buy a terrible looking hotdog, and then we pressed on until we were on the edges of a huge open space. No barriers, no ticket gates, no security - just lots of stalls, lots of people, and (to no great surprise) lots of beer. In the far distance a brightly illuminated stage housed a band beneath dazzling strobe lighting as they tore through a frenetic rock song with a swarm of people swaying around in front. Our lanky leader took this moment to flick his sunglasses that had been resting on top of his head, so that they were now in the classic eye-covering position. It was evidently time for business. We headed further into the action across the parched summer grass, the thud of the bass drum reverberating up through our legs and making our already unsteady progress that bit more challenging. We weaved through crowds of rowdy festival-goers until our trendy guide suddenly stopped outside of a particularly flashy looking marquee. He engaged in a brief conversation with a very serious looking man in a suit (who by coincidence was also wearing sunglasses), before embarking on a series of bizarre handshakes. We were then ushered through a red velvet curtain and up a ramp.

Before we could question where we were, a beer landed in each of our hands. Around us in all directions were glamorous women in sleek dresses, they're necks, ears, wrists and fingers all bathed in sparking jewellery. Men in suits hovered around them, adopting casual leans against the edge of the bar as they tried to engage them in no-doubt sophisticated conversation. And then there was us: a group of scruffy, slightly confused backpackers looking very out of place. Yes, I'm afraid even with my stylish new £1.50 t-shirt I was doing little to help us fit in here. But that wasn't what was occupying my thoughts right then, because as I shuffled through the forest of flashy suits I realised we were up on some sort of balcony overlooking the revellers below, and with a prime viewing spot of the stage, upon which the band's lead guitarist was now embarking on a mesmerising solo. I stood gazing out for a few minutes, having adopted my own swanky lean, but this was more out of balancing necessity than an attempt at a fashionable pose. This really was an impressive event, and not least because it was so vast and yet free, and somehow we had ended up in what appeared to be the VIP section. Our host was by now nowhere to be seen, but soon one of the other members of the group showed up beside me with some more drinks, and so we happily carried on the festivities unaided.

Chapter 21

Belgrade to Zagreb

I was woken by a sharp light burning down on my eyelids from above. I tilted my head sideways and buried my head as much as I could into the thin pillow in an attempt to evade its glare. The bed frame then creaked as I grudgingly swung around into a seating position. I looked up to find the source of this early morning inconvenience and saw that the fierce rays of the sun were reflecting off the silver blades of the scissors as they continued to precariously prop open the skylight above my head. Perhaps it had been best that I hadn't been too aware of my surroundings given that this is what I'd slept under all night. I say *all* night, but in fact it can't have been much more than four hours. I'd like to be able to tell you more about *Beerfest*, but I'm afraid it was all a bit hazy. I did find the faded remnants of an ink stamp on the back of my hand though, so it must have been good.

I dragged myself into the shower, humming what I assume were the distinctive melodic phrases of *Turbofolk* as the cool water splashed over my shoulders. I then found other additions to my skin as I felt the unmistakable bumps and itches of bites up my arm. After packing up my belongings I dropped my key off with the friendly lady at reception and thanked her for the excellent hospitality. She had been very friendly and sociable the previous evening, and so as I left I told her that I would recommend the hostel. She in turn said that she would recommend me as a guest. Travel is all about reciprocation.

Clinging to the Rails

As I made my way back to the station to begin the penultimate leg of my train trip, I stopped off at a kiosk to purchase a sandwich. I indicated which one I wanted to the lady behind the counter, and then was a little taken aback by the response I got.

'No! Not fresh!' the lady snapped, clearly very angry that I would dare to try and give her money for something that she was supposedly selling.

I shrugged and walked away. This experience along with the sweeping incident and the scissor-latch system adopted by the hostel left me with quite a mixed view of Serbia's approach to health and safety.

Despite this I was disappointed not to be sticking around longer in Belgrade as it had the feel of a city firmly on the up, and I'm sure it would prove a fascinating place to further explore, not to mention good value. In fact as I clambered aboard the rickety carriage ready to set off on the long journey to Zagreb, I found more than half the money I had originally taken out still in my wallet. I jokingly thought to myself that I should have used it to upgrade to first class to try and use up the now redundant currency. As it happened that would have been a very smart move.

I had been very cold throughout the journey on the night train from Budapest. Clinging to my own body to try and retain any semblance of heat as I shivered away had proved exhausting (although annoyingly not to the point I got any serious sleep), but this was hard to imagine as I sat in the cramped compartment in amongst five local men as we waited for the train to depart for the Croatian capital. It was already breaking past 30 degrees, and with no air conditioning we were relying on the frustratingly small gap provided by the semi-jammed drop-down window to ventilate the space. Just before the train rolled out of the station, triggering a slight but very welcome bit of air circulation through the musty compartment, a very smartly turned-out women entered and took the last remaining seat. She had immaculate hair and a silk scarf neatly wrapped around her neck, as well as a permanent smile fixed across her brightly lip-stick-clad face. I wondered if she had ever worked as an air hostess.

Once the train got up to speed (which wasn't as fast as I would have hoped), a ticket inspector slid open the door to our compartment. The men took it in turns to hand over their tickets without so much as a glance at the train official. The lady countered this by looking deep into his eyes as he passed her back her ticket, and said what sounded like, 'voila'. I handed over my ticket for inspection. I had now used up all of my train journey allocations on my InterRail pass and so I'd had to splash out around 12 pounds on this train journey north-west through the Balkans. I was actually relieved that I no longer needed to fill in all the details on the InterRail pass, as the juddery, swaying carriage and hot conditions wouldn't have made it easy. There was certainly no little drop-down wood-effect table on this service to lean on, either. He gave the ticket a quick scan and then held it back out to me. I decided to show my gratitude as well as my cheerful and considerate nature by imitating the lady opposite.

'Voila!' I said, smiling at the man.

The inspector stared suspiciously at me, and the lady with the scarf shot me a distrusting look. I hoped I hadn't just called him 'handsome' or something. I quickly took my ticket back and faced the floor. As I would later discover, *hvala* means 'thank you'. Well, I was *quite* close.

The hours dragged on as we skimmed alongside yellow corn fields in the hot afternoon sunshine. I pulled out my book in an attempt to distract myself from being buffeted between the two men on either side of me as the train veered around bends or rumbled over points systems, the irritation from the bites on my arms growing with each broken sleeper we bounced off. At just before four in the afternoon we crawled into Zagreb station, seven and a half hours after leaving Belgrade. The only other interruption to the quiet but heated trip had been the round of passport checks as we were stamped out of Serbia and then into Croatia, which was marked on my passport with a neat little steam engine symbol to show our method of arrival.

I appreciate that these last two journeys may not have really sold the idea of train travel to you, but I still maintain that these are some of the more memorable experiences, and they make arriving in each new destination that much more rewarding. Yes I was hot and tired, but within seconds of coming to a halt at the platform I had grabbed my bag from the rack above my seat, escaping the repressive environment of the compartment and was walking along a wide pavement in the centre of the city with a cool breeze sweeping over my face. I had booked my accommodation on the internet before my lively night out in Belgrade, and having glanced at a map of Zagreb online I'd had to make a quick decision as to whether to go for a hostel north of the station or one to the south. I'd decisively gone with one to the south, reckoning from my brief scan of the limited online map that this seemed like it was closer to the action, aided by the 98 per cent location rating that it had been given on the booking website.

Now I was here, it was clear that I'd made the wrong choice. Evidently those responsible for reviewing this hostel were massive fans of withdrawing money, and possibly little else. During the 10-minute walk along a main road running parallel to the train tracks on the southern side of the station I passed nine ATMs. I'll admit that coming across the first one was very convenient, as often I've found myself stranded in a new country without any legal currency, but I certainly didn't have enough in my account to be able to use each one I walked past here. Other than a healthy supply of cash machines the road was lined with characterless office blocks – banks, I cleverly deduced – and I was getting a little concerned that it felt like the last place you'd expect to find a hostel. I hoped that I hadn't misread the instructions of how to find the place, or worse, booked a hostel in a different city or country after a few too many 'welcome beers' in my Serbian residence.

Thankfully I hadn't, and as I turned off into a side road a few minutes later, I soon came across a small awning above a doorway with a couple of chairs and tables laid out in front of it. Inside was a lively little reception area. A man was sat on a stool playing music with a heavy beat from his laptop (I didn't know what it was, but it certainly wasn't Turbofolk) and another guy in combat-coloured shorts and a sleeveless vest was sat up at counter, behind which a girl with jet-black hair, a nose piercing and heavily tattooed arms sat. She greeted me with a big tongue-studded smile, and quickly checked me in. I was now just waiting for her to give me my room key so I could grab a shower and then pass out in my bed. I'd had no more than six hours sleep in three days and I was exhausted.

'Oh, I must get you your free shot!' she suddenly said.

I didn't want a free shot; I wanted sleep.

'Peter! You want a shot?' she shouted at the man on the stool as she reached for a grimy, unbranded two-litre plastic bottle from a shelf behind her.

I *really* didn't want a free shot. Peter shrugged and continued staring at his computer screen.

'What are you doing?' she said, postponing her move to retrieve the bottle of brown liquid and instead putting her hands on her hips in mock anger. Peter ignored her and changed the song.

For *goodness sake*, leave miserable Peter alone and *give me the room key*!

'It's okay, I don't need a shot' I interrupted, hoping this would speed proceedings along. She looked upset.

'No, I give you a shot – it's great!' she insisted.

Based upon its colour and packaging there was nothing to indicate that this was true.

'You want another shot?' she asked the vested one. He laughed and made some snide comment that went completely over my head, but it was enough to trigger the girl on reception to throw a small piece of stationery at him.

I sighed as the two of them got into a petty exchange whilst I stood awkwardly next to the counter, still patiently awaiting the shot I didn't want.

With an over-pronounced sigh the girl eventually gave up harassing the other hostelites and turned around, angrily grabbing the bottle from the shelf. She unscrewed the lid and immediately the air around my eyes started rippling. I then felt my eyes well up with tears and my nose muscles contract. The stench of the mystery liquid had not furthered my enthusiasm for this freebie. Nevertheless she pulled out a dirty shot glass from a draw beneath the counter and poured a healthy (or rather unhealthy) amount of the offending substance into it. I took a deep breath, grabbed the glass and threw the contents down my throat. I managed to suppress the urge to spit it immediately back out, and instead let out a gurgled cough. This seemed to make the girl happy, even if my expression would have given no such reason for her to feel this, but, in true *Crystal Maze*-esq style, the much coveted room key was then finally released to me.

Upstairs I showered and then headed down to the kitchen to get a drink of water. I'd thoroughly brushed my teeth to remove the foul taste of the shot from my mouth as best as I could, but I still felt that I needed something else to further wash it down with. After gulping down several glassfuls I noticed another staircase beyond the numerous cupboards that lined the wall. I made my way down the creaking stairs where I found a basement filled with large sofas. There was also a big television screen and a Texan in the corner. I'd been wondering where all the Americans had gone. I collapsed into one of the sofas and lay incapacitated from tiredness, fatigue and the restricting yet comforting density of cushioning I was now embroiled in.

'Hey, do you want the rest of this candy bar? I don't trust it' the Texan enquired with a thick Southern drawl.

No, I *didn't* want the rest of his chocolate bar. Why did people here feel the need to try and siphon off their crap to me? I eventually mustered the strength and will to drag myself out of the cushions and head up to bed. I really hoped that the next day would prove less demanding.

Chapter 22

Zagreb, Croatia

I had a decent night's sleep, which helped restore me to a suitable level of exploratory enthusiasm, so I was soon up and out of the hostel. I headed back along cash-machine alley and up past the station, continuing north towards the Old Town. It seemed to be very quiet for a capital city, but perhaps that's because the city is not the country's main visitor draw. Croatia benefits from an extensive and picturesque coastline that runs along the Adriatic Sea, where a number of attractive fortified towns swell up in the summer months with people looking to sample the coast's beaches and coves in the hot Southern European climate. These destinations (that are now heavily served by budget airlines) also act as bases for sailing trips to explore the many islands that sit just off the mainland. Zagreb is firmly inland however, and whilst it may not have any alluring beaches or spectacular sea views, it does have *a lot* of museums. I know this because I saw a sign (it would have been difficult to have missed it given its size) that gave arrows towards no less than 22 of them. This was one informative city.

The Lower Town is laid out in a not-especially inspiring grid formation, although the section immediately north of the station has a number of pleasant self-contained green areas, with curving pathways flanked by colourful flower beds and water features that add variation to the rows of buildings on either side. I walked up past the grand, sandy-yellow exterior of the glass-domed Art Pavilion and towards a scaffold-clad cathedral, where the streets became narrower and less regimented as I went up hill and entered the appropriately named Upper Town. I turned off the main street and walked through to a market square full of stalls selling an eclectic mix of handmade wooden crafts. Bright sunshine was supplying 30-plus degree heat; a factor that no doubt helps makes the beaches in this country so appealing (but less so the museums), whereas here it was mildly inconvenient as its dazzling rays reflected off the bright white-washed walls and vibrant red tiling of the buildings. I made my way through to a cobbled courtyard beneath a building that had mosaic crests worked into the tiles, and just beyond this I came across a small sign next to a doorway. Perhaps unsurprisingly, it was for a museum.

As previously mentioned; I'm not always that inclined to go into museums, but there are some situations that will sway me. Firstly, I might have had a strong recommendation, as was the case with the *Anne Frank Museum*, which certainly proved to be a worthwhile experience. Secondly, if it's very cold and/or wet outside I find that museums can be a welcome form of shelter, and wandering around exhibitions that threaten to teach you something about the world has got to be better than cowering under a bus stop shelter. And the third reason I will go into a museum is if there is something incredibly intriguing about it. I had not been recommended this museum (I had never heard of it, and shockingly it wasn't even one of the 22 that was listed on the sign I'd passed earlier), and it certainly wasn't cold or wet. It was in fact the intriguing name that encouraged me to push open the door of the *Museum of Broken Relationships*.

I wasn't too sure what I was expecting from it, but judging by the friendly lady behind the ticket desk and the brightly coloured souvenirs on display, I didn't see how it could be as downbeat as the name suggested. I handed over a few Croatian Kunas and headed into the exhibition. If I thought the name was intriguing, this was nothing compared to what I found on the various shelves and cabinets around the small rooms and corridors inside. The museum is a collection of objects, each with a brief description or story next to it of what it symbolised in a failed relationship. Some of the objects are simple items, such as a letter sent overseas, an item of clothing left behind or a trinket once held in high regard that over time became an unhappy reminder. Some descriptions took the form of a heart-felt tale to highlight the object's significance, such as the poetic description that accompanied the 'divorce day dwarf', whilst some had a more light-hearted sentiment, with humorous back-stories as to why they came to mean what they did and ultimately end up in this bizarre but fascinating collection. Some of the objects were just concerning, such as the axe (labelled the 'ex-axe'), which was apparently used to chop up the furniture of a former partner. I suppose it was endearing in its own special way. The objects have been donated from across the world, although mainly from around the Balkans, Germany and - slightly unexpectedly - the Philippines, although I later discovered that this was because the museum had toured around selective parts of the world, and had spent a while out in the Philippines collecting items.

I ended up spending quite some time working my way around the small museum with its eclectic mix of objects as I read each of the tales of international encounters. The detailed accounts they gave – or sometimes just brief glimpses of a story – for me highlighted the real significance that other people can have on travel experiences. Travelling solo is often the most sociable way of seeing the world, as the countless fleeting interactions you inevitably have may not seem significant at the time, but ultimately they are the moments that so often shape your memories and perceptions of a place, and distinguish it from yet another visit to a castle. These moments may not always dictate your travels (although judging by these museum stories and some of my previous experiences they certainly can do), but they decorate it - like the sprinkles on a cake, or maybe the layer of jam in between the sponge layers. I don't know, I'm not very good at metaphors (and I think I had cake on my mind after seeing one of the more culinary-based museum exhibits), but there's no doubting the effect that others can have on your journey, whatever your reasons for being on it. Perhaps most significantly is that I've found these moments to be most prevalent on the move between places, where the excitement and anticipation of a new destination is at its strongest, and where you're often at your most open to influence as you head into the unknown. I've also found that no form of transport is more conducive to this than train travel.

I left the *Museum of Broken Relationships* more cheered than I would have expected given the name. A little further along the street I was then further cheered by the emergence of a small bell tower in the same white brick and stone as the neighbouring buildings. It wasn't especially tall, but having negotiated the collection of disjointed and rickety staircases up to the open-air observation level, I was treated to far-reaching views thanks to its position on the edge of the Upper Town. I gazed out over the city stretching out to the south, scanning the flat, hazy horizon, and then I walked around the circular platform to the other side, from where I could see lush green hills to the north. A sign inside explained how the Lotrščak Tower (from the Latin, meaning 'bell of thieves') was built to defend the Upper Town, which was then called Gradec, and was rung to signify the closing of the town gates. Later it housed a canon to mark the time for the residents of the surrounding area, and to this day a canon is fired everyday at noon. Unfortunately I had missed today's firing because of my museum commitments. More insightful than this sign though, was the placard that informed me that the best time of year to visit Zagreb was in winter, summer, spring or autumn. It was very reliving to know that I'd timed my trip so well.

I returned to the Lower Town courtesy of yet another little funicular railway (which I was convinced took longer than if I'd walked) and decided to congratulate myself on visiting the city during the perfect season with a refreshing beverage. I found a quiet restaurant just beyond the lower station of the funicular railway and sat under a wide awning that stretched out across the cobbled street. After briefly scanning the menu I ordered what sounded like the perfect drink, combining as it did two of my favourite alcoholic and non-alcoholic flavours: beer and lemon. It was in fact a lemon beer! It quickly arrived and I took a sip. It was horrible.

I was beginning to feel tired again as I sat outside the hostel a little later, sipping a coke to try and restore my energy and my faith in the drinks industry. I had my book out, but I wasn't paying much attention to the pages. It was so tempting to head upstairs and lie down, but I was determined not to waste the rest of the day. In just a few days I would be back home to start my new job, and so I was now very aware that I should make the most of this time to explore these places that I'd travelled all this distance to see.

Beyond the table where I was sitting I noticed a collection of rather dilapidated looking bicycles. At first it hadn't occurred to me that they might be for hire, but after gulping down the rest of my drink I made a quick enquiry inside at the hostel reception desk, and soon I emerged with a key. It was a bit of a faff trying to extract the rusty frame that loosely held together what was to be my designated bike, but after some determined twisting and yanking of metal hoops I finally released it from the mangled rack. I lined it up beside the kerb and climbed on.

I decided to head further south, in part to vindicate my accidental decision to base myself on the wrong side of the city, but also because I had spotted the distinctive curve of a river from when I was at the top of the Lotrščak Tower. I set off through the residential streets that backed on to the hostel, wobbling along as I tried to adapt to the bizarre upright seating position that this strange bicycle forced me to adopt. It was certainly different from the mountain bike I was used to back home. Thankfully the roads were deserted, and so I was safe to meander about across the tarmac, trying to control the rattling contraption as the chain crunched along in desperate need of an oiling. Aside from the handlebars curving around to the side, I also became aware of a distinct lack of a brake lever. It was a shame that I hadn't noticed this before reaching the end of a cul de sac, as it wasn't until after I'd bounced painfully up a kerb and hit the wheelie bin that I worked out that you had to pedal *backwards* to brake. Thankfully, with little more than a bruised ego, I quickly brushed myself off and got back on the bicycle. Ironically the accident seemed to help cure the excessive rattling as I trundled along a pathway that led up some steep grass banking to the edge of the Rijeka Sava.

The temperature had dropped to a far more amicable level as evening set in, and the cool breeze blowing along the top of the sizeable riverbank made for a very calm and pleasant setting. I could see a few other people strolling along the opposing bank, whilst overhead the sun drifted in between thin clouds as it cast a reddening glow that was reflected in the wide, smooth surface of the water. Having more or less got to grips with the bike, I headed east along the gravel path on top of the bank, my earlier tiredness spinning away with every rotation of the pedals. I followed the gentle curve of the river until I came to a bridge that I crossed over. In the distance I caught sight of the distinctive shape of a modern stadium, adjacent to some other large but equally architecturally striking buildings. I dropped down off the south bank of the river and followed what looked like a newly built road, crossing under a busy highway where I came out next to what turned out to be a shopping centre next to the stadium. I found a rack, locked up the bike and wandered over. The whole area looked like it had recently been regenerated, with the crisp glass and steel encased buildings set amongst patches of thoughtfully landscaped planting still yet to properly bed in. I walked through a square where fountains shot out of grills in the paving, much to the entertainment of some children who were busy running in and out of them as they tried to avoid getting caught out by the sudden bursts of water. Further along there was a makeshift beach volleyball court that had been set up for elder fun-seekers, and dotted about were benches filled with weary shoppers who were taking a short break from lugging about their heavy bags. I found a little supermarket near the entrance of the shopping centre and grabbed some food that I took back up to the riverbank. I sat on the grass and munched on my edible offerings in the peaceful surrounds as the sun slowly set behind me.

As I finished off my riverside cuisine, the onset of dusk brought an unwelcome guest in the form of a swarm of midges. They emerged in an aggressive cluster around my head and began harassing me as I sat on the grassy bank. I took this as a sign to leave, so I collected the bike and set off back towards the bridge. As I regained my balance on the uncomfortable saddle, I passed a couple that were being hotly pursued by a little black dog. When I approached it took a sudden interest in the spokes of my wheels, and began excitably jumping in and around the frame whilst I tried desperately not to run it over. I stopped, fearing my lack of coordination on the bike and this dog's reckless enthusiasm for my wheels could only end badly, and waited for the couple to move along and take their dog with them. Strangely though, as the pair disappeared behind the wall of an overpass without so much as a backward glance, the dog continued to jump about next to me. I slowly pushed off in the opposite direction, assuming an affectionate call would soon cut through the evening air, triggering the little animal to scurry off happily towards its owners. But this didn't happen. Instead the dog started following me, bounding along with a slightly odd sideways stance as its little pink tongue hung out of its mouth. It appeared that this dog had come out alone this evening. I carried on along the pathway, constantly looking back to see what the dog was doing. It was still following me, although it appeared to be struggling to keep up as it only had little legs. I felt guilty about leading it astray, but I wasn't sure what else I should do, so I maintained a slower pace.

Colin (which is the name I gave to him (or her), because I've never owned a dog and have no idea of what a good name for a dog is) kept in hot pursuit. I maintained my relaxed pace as little Colin continued to hurry along behind. He briefly stopped when he encountered a stray cat that arched its back menacingly at him, but then he realised that I was still peddling along ahead, and so he brushed off the distraction and carried on the chase. After about 10 minutes I was starting to get a little concerned at how committed he was to sticking with me. I even wondered if they would charge me for an extra guest at the hostel if he made it all the way back, and he'd never be able to handle the free shot. It was then that I passed under a bridge, weaving around torn cardboard boxes and various bits of discarded junk. I came out of the other side and looked back, but Colin was nowhere to be seen. It was now almost pitch black, and I suddenly felt guilty at having unwittingly led him out to a deserted bridge in the dark. I then realised that I was a loan traveller standing about by a deserted bridge in the dark, and so with little obvious alternative I got back on the bike and carried on. When I arrived back at the hostel I was amazed to only get charged two

Euros for the bike hire. This was both remarkable in its cheapness, and also by the fact that this was not a legal currency in Croatia. I headed to bed, satisfied with my day's achievements.

Chapter 23

Zagreb to Ljubljana

I woke up sharply the following morning having had a horribly graphic dream about a Beethoven-esq dog kidnapping. I quickly brushed this aside and got up and ready to go, as it was time to set off on my final train journey of the trip.

For a moment it looked like I wouldn't be leaving Zagreb as quickly as I'd anticipated. I was sat on the train in a full compartment ready to go when it began pulling out of the station. The only problem was, we didn't leave with it. The front half of the train set off, whilst the rear half remained firmly routed in the station. I looked around perplexed at this odd development, as did the others, which was of some relief. A few minutes later we also set off, apparently in pursuit of the front of the train in what I can only assume is some bizarre Croatian railway game.

It was cooler onboard this train than the one I had arrived on, although each of the six seats in the compartment were taken. It may have been a little crowded (although strangely quiet) in the carriage, but this final leg was a mere two hours, and so I was more than happy to sit back and embrace this last rail exploit before I became a miserable and embittered train commuter back in London. We rattled along as we made our way west towards the border, where we stopped to have our passports checked. The Croatian official seemed less interested in our identification though, and was far keener to check under the seats, presumably for hidden contraband – drugs maybe, or perhaps little black dogs. Satisfied we weren't trying to smuggle any illicit substances over the border, we continued to the Slovenian checkpoint. I've never quite understood the gap between leaving one country and being stamped into the next. I always fear that something bad could happen, like having a magazine thrown in my face, and we wouldn't be under any country's legal jurisdiction for the perpetrator to be punished. Here I was again in the land-equivalent of international waters; a weird kind of limbo state of uncertainty. Thankfully, none of my co-travellers looked like the magazine-throwing types, and soon we had stopped again for the Slovenian side of proceedings. The door was thrown open with such ferocity that we all jumped slightly.

'Passport!' the short, angry-faced lady with a gun shouted.

We all swiftly held them out for her. She was very wide (partly due to all the weapons she had strapped around her waist) and so she had to turn sideways to fit through the narrow doorway of the compartment as she snatched our documents for scrutiny. She studied each face and its corresponding photograph with a distrusting eye. I smiled dumbly when she got to me, which seemed to irritate her enough to throw my passport back into my lap with a look of disdain, before she turned her attention to the Japanese man next to me.

'Where you from?' she barked, her sharp tone causing him to recoil slightly in his seat.

'Er…J-Japan' he stuttered.

Told you.

'Empty your bag!'

He did as he was told, quickly loosening the straps of his backpack ready to have his belongings flung about by the female officer's comparatively weedy male assistant. While this went on she laid into the poor Japanese guy with a barrage of classic border-control questions: 'Where are you going? How long are you staying? 'What's the name of Jupiter's largest moon?'

Once they were finished with him they did the same to the Dutch girl on the opposite seat. I felt sorry for them having to answer these demeaning and frankly rather pointless questions, as well as going through the embarrassment and hassle of emptying and re-packing their bags - apparently just for being of a certain nationality. This was by far the fiercest border crossing I had faced on my trip (which was slightly ironic as since my visit Croatia has joined the EU, and so this border is now free to cross. Perhaps this patrol guard was just angry because she knew she was losing her job).

There was a marked shift in the scenery as we went further into Slovenia. The flat land we had been crossing was starting to undulate, and our relatively straight-line routing was beginning to meander in line with this changing topography. Soon we were carving through deep valleys covered in dense forest. I got up and left the crowded train compartment and joined a number of others who were assembling in the corridor to get a closer look at the exciting change in landscape. A river was weaving in and out beneath the train track as we crossed over bridges and skirted around deep gorges. Quaint little churches occasionally punctured the rich greenery, with their towers marking peaks as they stood watch over the neatly ploughed fields that stretched out precariously on the steep mountainous slopes below. It was nice to stretch my legs after the confined space of the compartment, and being able to feel the breeze against my face through the windows added to the enjoyment of the dramatic scenes outside. After a while the land began to flatten out again, and then it wasn't long before people began disappearing back into their compartments to collect up their bags. I sensed our arrival in Ljubljana was imminent.

Chapter 24

Ljubljana, Slovenia

I was feeling a little nostalgic as we pulled up into Ljubljana station at the end of what was my final train journey on this summer trip across Europe. I'd covered hundreds of miles through numerous countries; crossing a variety of terrain whilst taking in some fascinating cities and meeting a number of interesting and bizarre characters along the way. And now here I was at my final destination - the Central Slovenian city of Ljubljana, in the Balkan North-West of South-East Europe. I patted the side of the carriage as I stepped down onto the platform, thinking about all the trains I'd climbed on and off, each one full of excitement and anticipation at what the next journey and new city might bring. More than ever this journey across Western, Northern, Central, Eastern and Southern Europe had underlined for me just how much being on the move, and that element of the unknown about what was ahead, was what I really loved about travelling. I then quickly decided that train-patters are probably frowned upon in Slovenia, and so I stopped my moment of introspection and focused on the fact that I had one last city to explore.

The streets were quiet around the station, and the urban scene seemed a little dreary, especially after the dramatic surroundings I'd come through on the journey from Zagreb. I feared it was going to be a bit of a flat ending to my trip, and my bland hostel in an indistinct concrete block around the corner gave little indication things were set to improve. I battled with the sheets as I made up my creaky metal-framed lower bunk (something I wouldn't miss having to do almost every morning), and then I set off armed with a map the hostel had kindly provided, hoping there was a part of the city more worthy of exploring than the small excerpt I'd seen so far.

I walked along a narrow street that branched off the main road and emerged into a pleasant little square, or more accurately, a pleasant little circle. The quiet, unmemorable streets that I'd been walking through were suddenly replaced with a flourish of activity, which was set against an incredibly picturesque riverside scene. The 'square' had patterned cobbles that stretched out from the centre in a circular formation. A pinky-red and white church stood as the centrepiece overlooking the circular square, with a succession of bridges on the opposing side offering a generous number of options for crossing the narrow river that was flowing beneath them. Promenades wound off around the bends along each side of the river, and on this hot summer's day there were large canvas awnings stretching out from the walls of adjacent cafés and restaurants engulfing them. Beneath their expansive cover were trestle tables packed with people who were indulging in various enticing refreshments as they soaked up the pleasant surroundings. Another unavoidable element of this picture-postcard scene was a steeply banked tree-covered hill on the other side of the river, upon which the unmistakable shapes of castle ramparts were poking up above the rich green canopy. I know, I know – another European city, another castle. I would have put my limited remaining Euros on there being a funicular railway in the near vicinity, too, but before finding out I decided to first take a walk along the river.

As I passed the first outdoor café I realised that there was something unusual about one of the tables. Where as most of them were filled with cups or glasses, often in close proximity to small plates with appetising cakes on them, this particular one had a board game on it. Either side of the table were sat two men, each with a high level of concentration on their face as they stared at the black and white squares in front of them. More unusual still was the video camera set up on a tripod behind them, its lens focusing on the table in the middle. Every few seconds one of the men would make a swift hand movement over the top of the board, before quickly tapping a little clock beside it. As a couple of people moved out of the way I noticed a sign next to the gamers. I moved in closer, and discovered that I was in fact witnessing the early stages of a world record attempt at the longest chequers match. It had begun at 10 o'clock that morning, and was set to finish at 10 o'clock tomorrow morning. That was unquestionably a lot of chequers, but whilst it may be an unusual spectacle, looking around I couldn't imagine too many nicer settings in which to undertake such a challenge.

As well as the endless selection of food and drink outlets there were also a number of stalls dotted along the waterside promenade. Each was selling a selection of tasteful trinkets, such as locally crafted jewellery and landscape watercolour paintings of the city, as well as one selling a range of puzzles that were keeping a number of passer-bys entertained. I was again feeling a little weary, but in a more pleasant, calm sort of way. I stopped off at one of the outdoor ice cream counters and then found a spot down by the water. As I sat lazily licking my lemon sorbet ice cream, my brain turned to thoughts of my impending new employment.

In less than 48 hours I would be sat at my new desk in central London, probably battling with an onslaught of bizarre acronyms and phraseology that had been thrown at me during my first few hours of a stressful and unnerving morning. I would no doubt be wading through a vast number of emails that had arrived before me and that I didn't understand thanks to someone having 'thoughtfully' added me to a ridiculous number of email groups that currently meant nothing to me. I'd also be desperately trying to remember *even one* person's name from the 45 second window in which I'd been introduced to everyone on the floor, whilst simultaneously trying to figure out how I should be dressed, based on what everyone else (or at least the male contingent) was wearing. A shirt? A tie? Novelty pink and green striped socks?! And all this after a potentially strenuous first commute (of no doubt many) on the wondrously overcrowded and unreliable train network.

I had so much to look forward to, but right now none of that mattered, because here I was sitting on a ledge dangling my bare feet over the cooling water of the Ljubljanica River, eating an ice cream in the sunshine. But all good things must come to an end, and so as the last of my ice cream dribbled onto my shoe, I stood up, wiped my mouth, and got ready to see one last castle. I crossed over one of the many bridges and headed back along the east side of the river, this time veering off into a narrow street running behind the café gauntlet. Mixed in amongst the colourfully painted buildings I found the pristine Town Hall in front of a fountain. A sign informed me that this was the Town Square, which again I will have to pull the local council up on, as this space was far more rectangular. Letting another basic mathematical slip go, I continued to follow the curving Ciril - Metodov Street until it opened out on to a large market square (which I was relived to find was genuinely square-shaped) where a number of stalls were making a swift trade from fresh Adriatic fish. Thankfully I had a map with me, as otherwise I would never had known that the way up to the castle was via a narrow footpath that disappeared behind a building at the back of the market, which then rose steeply upwards into the trees above. It was quite an effort to climb, especially in flip-flops that kept falling off as I lost my footing on tree roots and large stones that were scattered across the uneven pathway. A little breathless I finally made it to the summit, the dense greenery having strategically blocked out any views until I had gone through the castle gate, bought my eight Euro ticket and had climbed to the top of the main tower.

It would be safe to say that vertigo suffers would not envy this excursion. The narrow spiralling steps and the tight space around the top of the tower were not made with the faint-hearted in mind - not to mention the steep drop through the thick stone crenelations that offered a birds-eye view of the river and its café-covering awnings. But even those less inclined to seek the highest heights would still surely marvel at the mass of red, angular roofs, pastel beige and white coloured walls and dense greenery that flows off over the hills, slowly disappearing in the summer haze. It was from up here that I really noticed the compactness of the city. In some ways it felt like a compressed Prague, but with a fresh vibrancy that thrives on the fact it has yet to be fully exposed to the tourist masses.

The castle itself offers more than just a viewpoint. I took some time to have a look around the small but very informative museum that documents the turbulent history of the Balkans. The museum also has in it the world's oldest wooden wheel (with an axel), believed to date back to 3200 BC, which is a *wheely* long time ago, although as with Brussels' prize possession, this too was a replica, as the original is kept in the City Museum. In another corner of the castle I found a small, neatly appointed chapel, and on the other side of the courtyard was a café, an outdoor stage (that apparently hosts theatre and cinema nights) and there was even a modern art exhibition being held in the cool, darkened chambers that lurked beneath the walls. Ljubljana certainly knows how to get the most out of an attraction, and how to make the most efficient use of a space. As one final offering for those brave enough to hike up the hill, a mini outdoor library had been set up beneath a tree as part of a reading festival, where a mobile shelving unit invited people to pick up a book and go and sit on a nearby cushion to read. I chose a book with lots of nice pictures of the country, because my Slovenian still wasn't quite up to scratch, and also because I'm not seven years old anymore and so my teacher can't tell me off for just looking at the pictures.

I descended the castle hill (by yes, you guessed it – *another* funicular railway) and found a few more square squares to the west of the river. These included the spacious and park-adjacent Congress Square that has the Slovenian School Museum at one end, and the disappointingly drab Republic Square a further block over, where independence was declared on the 26 June 1991, but from what I saw was now being used as a car park. Satisfied that I had seen a balanced selection of Ljubljana's squares, I re-crossed the river, managing to find yet another bridge in this short section of river as I went in search of an early evening stomach filler. I found a makeshift stand from which I bought a freshly griddled chicken and pepper kebab that came with two chunky wedges of herb-baked bread. I happily ate up the tasty offering as darkness fell for the final time on my journey across the continent.

The night brought a scene change for central Ljubljana. Ice creams were no longer the refreshment of choice, as wine and beer were now flowing freely along the riverside tables. The glare of the sun had been replaced by the subtle orange glow of the lanterns that lit the Ljubljanica, whilst the gentle soundtrack of a live acoustic guitar drifted through the air. I wandered through the streets one more time to soak up the relaxed atmosphere, pausing at the numerous bridges that had now become stages for street entertainers. Appreciative crowds were clapping enthusiastically at the various fire-juggling routines, balancing acts and general costume-clad extravagances. This really was a very pleasant place to finish my trip. My creaky-framed bed was beckoning though, and so did London, and of course my new job. It was time to say goodnight to Ljubljana and prepare for my final one-way trip of the summer.

Chapter 25

Ljubljana to London

Before tracking down the bus that would take me to the airport, I took one last stroll along the river. It was Sunday morning, and a more formal atmosphere had replaced the lively and sociable scenes of the previous evening. I spotted a number of conservatively dressed locals making their way into the church, quietly pushing open the large wooden door and slipping into the darkness beyond. A few people were sat outside the cafés, but they were now sipping coffee as opposed to wine. On the other side of the square sat the two men, still nudging counters around the board and tapping the little timer as their world record attempt reached is climax, albeit with an added weariness that you would expect from having spent 23 hours playing the same repetitive game. There was a pile of lightly crushed energy drink cans building up beside them, that was evidence of the efforts they had needed to sustain this prolonged gaming, but with one hour to go they looked set to complete their challenge. I was sorry that I couldn't stick around to congratulate them, but ultimately I found watching them for more than 30 seconds a bit boring, and anyway, I had places to be. I zig-zagged along the river, crossing each bridge in turn before looping back through the cobbled streets beneath Castle Hill. It was then time to head back out of the quaintness of central Ljubljana and take up my position at the bus stop on the main road.

I was a little subdued as I sat at the back of the little airport bus as it trundled along through the indistinct suburbs of the Slovenian capital. I was disappointed to have reached the end of my trip, but I was also very satisfied (and quite frankly a little amazed) that I had managed to pack in as many stops as I did in the short amount of time I'd had available. There had been some close calls along the way, but ultimately the trains had served me well, and they really had given me a strong snapshot of the changing landscape of this eclectic and densely countrified continent.

Another reason I was feeling a little miserable was because of my impending return to the world of air travel. It had been great that I'd managed to find a cheap ticket back to London on which to blow my final few pennies, but the idea of being once again stuffed into a cramped, aged aeroplane did not appeal, and it certainly didn't hold much promise for a glamorous return to England to start my flash new job in the city.

Once at the airport I got my boarding pass quickly thanks to a friendly lady on the check-in desk. I whizzed through security and passport control and was soon sitting in the surprisingly empty departure lounge. I'd noted that it had been very quiet all around the terminal building, to the point where I felt the need to double-check my boarding pass to make sure that I'd got the right day (and airport). Thankfully everything seemed in order, but I was surprised to discover that there was a pre-assigned seat number on my ticket (which itself resembled a traditional laminated boarding pass - as opposed to a printout on a piece of paper). I'd never heard of the airline I was flying with, which had initially made me sceptical, but as I stepped on board after a very relaxed and orderly boarding process I found myself in what appeared to be a brand new plane. Far from being a crude budget offering, this aircraft (from what I found out was actually Slovenia's national carrier) was a well-presented and appealing sight – not unlike central Ljubljana. A smart (but not overly made-up) air hostess welcomed me aboard and directed me to my seat. I sat down and buckled up, marvelling at the impressive amount of leg room and plushness of the seat, with its smart, neutral blue and grey colour scheme. After a smooth take-off the cabin crew then moved swiftly along the aisle dispensing refreshments. I eyed the lady that stood above me with suspicion as she handed me a neatly packaged chicken wrap, just waiting for an out-stretched hand that would be demanding payment. But there wasn't one. They were providing *complimentary* food, and this was quickly followed by a free drink. This really was the high life.

The two-hour journey quite literally flew by, and soon I was queuing up at the busy immigration area at London Luton (which is of course is not especially near London) surrounded by masses of other UK returnees, who I noted all looked a lot wearier than I did (and I bet they had only visited one country). I guessed that most of them hadn't spent over 50 hours on trains either, yet there was an overwhelming mood of grumpiness and irritation in the musty post-holiday air as we all weaved around the barriers, slowly edging towards the security desks. As I waited, taking heed of the many signs requesting passports are removed from their protective holder (an irritating requirement that I find only exists at UK borders, and one that causes significant bending and creasing to my passport so that it effectively renders the protective cover useless) I flicked through its pages to look at some of the new stamps I had acquired from the non-EU countries that I'd visited on this journey. Each one brought back memories of the different trains and situations I'd collected them in. Airport passport checks all blur into one, but on this trip I had far more memorable border crossings; from being pulled out of the queue at St Pancras, woken by an eccentric Hungarian lady in the middle of the night and watching the thorough Slovenian border guard rummage through the other passengers' bags. Despite all being trains, there had been a lot of variation between the style and manner in which the journeys had taken place, as each had their own distinctive twists and quirks.

After around 20 minutes I stepped up to have my passport scanned, which is as definitive a mark as you can get of no longer being abroad (although not as definitive as a stamp would have been – but as I was once told, stamping a passport within EU bound flights would now apparently be a breech of human rights). On the bus back from the airport my thoughts moved from all the train journeys I'd been on lately to the one I had coming up the next morning. I knew it wasn't going to have the excitement of the international services that I'd been getting used to, and it certainly wouldn't feature the dramatic waterside scenes I'd encountered going up through Denmark, the open crop-filled fields of Croatia or the mountains of Slovenia, but I at least hoped it wouldn't be too crowded, or filled with unscheduled stops like the Hungarian night train had been. Basically I was feeling pretty unexcited about my next venture on the tracks, but as some consolation, at least I'd still be getting a discount with my 16 to 25 railcard.

Chapter 26

London, England

'Please note that railcards are not valid on rush hour services.'

I stood motionless for a few seconds, staring dumbly at the ticket machine. I'd dragged myself out of bed unnecessarily early, put on clothes that would no doubt prove to be overly smart and I'd got down to the station in plenty of time to buy my discounted ticket. But no, apparently I wasn't allowed to use my railcard. I grudgingly stuffed some notes into the slot to purchase my painfully expensive ticket and headed up to the platform. The previous evening I'd chosen the 8.05 as the service that should get me into Central London ready to tackle the gauntlet of the London Underground. On the departure screen above the platform it said that it was on time. I walked along to the far end of the platform on the basic assumption that there would be more space in the carriages, weaving through the other commuters until they thinned in number. At 8.06 the screen changed to 'Expected 8.07', and then at 8.09 the train emerged from around a bend in the distance and slowed as it drew up alongside the platform. The suited men and women that had been nonchalantly reading newspapers or sipping coffees suddenly converged on the platform edge – each seeming to know the exact point at which their favoured doors would eventually come to a stop. They had their routines, and no doubt soon I would have mine.

As the morning sun was cut out by the newly arrived train I could just about see through the heavily tinted windows of the carriages. What I saw was not inviting, because the train was *packed*. I sighed and joined the rabble lined up beside the nearest carriage, waiting for the beeps that would signal the opening of the doors and the commencement of the boarding free-for-all. I'd hoped that perhaps lots of these people would be getting off, but no, everyone wanted to be in Central London. I allowed the more desperate passengers to push on first, and then I hesitantly raised one foot up into the carriage and hauled myself in.

It felt like we were stood there for an age as people edged about trying to claim any morsel of extra space they could. A little foot shuffle here, a repositioned arm there; this was silent, calculating spatial warfare. Eventually there was another round of beeps and the doors closed, triggering a collective release of breath as everyone readjusted having had the confirmation that no more passengers would be boarding. Thankfully there were no more stops until we reached the train's final destination. I rested back against the doors to relieve the pressure on my chest caused by the backpack of another commuter being pressed tightly up against me. A man then reached out to rest his hand against the doorframe to steady himself as the train began to edge out of the station. I now had an arm rubbing up against my face and the threat of an already damp armpit in dangerous proximity. The lady next to me then attempted to turn the page of her newspaper, the corners of the thin sheets nicking sharply against my cheek as she did so. The man with the backpack then fell back against me as we were unceremoniously thrown around a bend in the tracks, with the small, newly created space ahead of him immediately snatched up in a quick lunge by a lady in a floral dress. I was now firmly wedged in. This was my life now. This is how every morning would begin. I let out a resigned breath - or at least as far as my compressed diaphragm would allow. At least I only had to endure 17 minutes of this.

There was a sudden jolt followed by heavy breaking as the train came to an abrupt and uncomfortable stop. The engine cut out, and then a few seconds later a crackly voice from the speaker above my head broke the newly formed silence.

'Please be aware that due to signal problems on the line there will be delays to this service.'

Or maybe not.

I am still yet to see my picture appear on the 'drawings of the month' section of the *Statens Museum for Kunst* website. I live in hope.

And there was no sign of a mouse. It must have been the boiler.

Author's Note

Whilst *clinging to the rails* I passed through 14 countries. Because of the fleeting nature of the trip, the language skills I developed were...*selective*. I did learn a few words though, and they predominantly mean 'thank you'. At least I hope they do, or I may not be very welcome in a lot of places anymore. So, to all those that I met along the way and who helped keep my journey on track...

Thank you, merci, dank u, tak, tack, takk, danke, děkuji, ďakujem, köszönöm, хвала, hvala!

Basically, I'm very grateful.

That's it, I'm afraid.